THRIVE!

Kingdom Precepts for Maximised Living

Volume 2

Yemi Akinsiwaju

© 2022

THRIVE!
Kingdom Precepts for Maximised Living

Volume 2

First published in Great Britain by Dayspring Publishing
Copyright © Yemi Akinsiwaju 2022
First published in paperback in 2022

The rights of Yemi Akinsiwaju to be identified as the author of the Work has been asserted by him in accordance with the Copyright, Designs and Patents Act 1988.

All rights reserved. This book is protected by the copyright laws of the United Kingdom. No part of this publication may be used, distributed or reproduced by any means, graphic, electronic or mechanical, including photocopying, recording, taping or by any information storage retrieval system without the prior written permission of the author except in the case of brief quotations embodied in critical articles or reviews.

ISBN (Paperback)   – 978-0-9934482-6-3
ISBN (Kindle)   – 978-0-9934482-7-0

Unless otherwise noted, Scripture quotations are taken from the Holy Bible, New King James Version®. Copyright © 1982, 1984 by Thomas Nelson, Inc.

To order additional copies of this book, contact:
Dayspring Publishing Ltd
Tel: +44 (0)208 469 3780
Email: orders@dayspringpublishing.com

DEDICATION

To you, my esteemed reader who seeks to live a life of significance and make a difference in our world.

To you who refuse to settle for average and dare to believe that God has placed in you a gift that ought to be released for the benefit of humanity.

I dedicate this book to you in the earnest hope that something you glean from within its pages will ignite the flames of greatness within you and cause you to thrive even more in the pursuit and fulfilment of your unique assignment to humanity.

Keep Soaring!

You Have Made A Difference.

Thank You!

By purchasing this book, you have donated towards enhancing the life of someone in need.

Profits from this book will go towards charitable causes including the work of the following organisations:

Idanre Development Foundation:

Dedicated to fighting poverty, facilitating educational development and raising the quality of life for the underprivileged in Idanre town, Nigeria.

International Third World Leaders Association:

Actively involved in transforming followers into leaders and leaders into agents of positive change in over 40 developing countries.

ACKNOWLEDGEMENTS

'No man is an island' is a self-evident truth that resonates particularly in the field of literary endeavours. Every book is a synthesis of ideas from many minds; this second volume of **Thrive** is no different. It is a product of the contributions of the various authors who penned the books of the Bible as the creator of the universe inspired them and the learnings from many other teachers whose insights have inspired me and helped me in my life's journey thus far… to them I say, "Thank You."

To my precious wife, Abi, thank you for all the lessons you have taught me in our journey together. To my beloved daughters, Oluwatosin, Toluwalope and Oluwaseun, thank you for continuing to manifest the greatness that God has placed within you… I love you all infinitely!

My wonderful parents, Emmanuel and Grace Akinsiwaju… thank you for being my first introduction to the many principles shared in this book, through the lives of purpose, integrity and love that you lived so eloquently. I love you always and forever.

To my beloved mentor, Dr Myles Munroe and your beautiful wife, Pastor Ruth, Thank you for your investments in my life. Your seeds of leadership and love continue to bear fruit… Forever grateful.

My New Wine Church Family… thank you for being a constant haven of hope, faith and love, empowering people around the world to discover, develop and deploy their unique potential to the glory of God. I love you.

To you, the reader, I salute your passion to pursue insights and ideas that will equip you to maximise your life and be a blessing to your generation.

Thank you for choosing '**Thrive**' as one of the tools to help propel you onwards and upwards in your quest.

Finally, to the source of ultimate truth and wisdom, God Almighty... Thank YOU!

Contents

Dedication v

Thank You. vii

Acknowledgements ix

Introduction 1

Insights 3

Other Resources 121

About the Author 125

References 127

INTRODUCTION

This is the second volume in my **Thrive** series. It is a compendium of insights gleaned from studying what I consider to be the most comprehensive, illuminating and extensively proven manual for effective living ever written – The Bible.

Many people erroneously treat the Book either as a collection for dogmatic religious devotions or as an irrelevancy to their lives in modern-day society… thereby unfortunately depriving themselves of the greatest asset for handling the intricacies of life in the most effective way possible.

I have personally found that within the pages of the Bible rest the ancient, yet evergreen wisdom for modern times. It provides the simple, yet profound and practical answers to the wide-ranging questions that affect every human life in areas of individual fulfilment, organisational success, community growth, national development and global harmony.

Every normal human seeks to live a happy, positive, fruitful life, regardless of your religious / spiritual persuasion or lack thereof. I am fully persuaded that the principles in the Bible will help you achieve such a life.

Thrive is written to introduce you to some of those foundational precepts that will radically transform your life for the better and hopefully, at some point, you will recognise that the ultimate author of those principles indeed wants you and every human to enjoy an incredibly blessed life.

I offer this volume with the earnest expectation that something you read in here will energize your spirit, ignite your passion and serve as a catalyst to unleash even more of the greatness that lies within you.

I also hope that **Thrive** will stimulate every reader, religious or non-religious, to approach the Bible with an open mind and unveil for yourself much more of those gems of life-transforming wisdom tucked within its pages.

I honour you and celebrate your quest for personal growth... may you fulfil your unique purpose to the glory of God and the benefit of humanity.

Keep Soaring!

Yemi Akinsiwaju

(The Leadership Catalyst)

INSIGHTS

THE QUESTION

One of the most fundamental questions every human must periodically consider and truthfully answer is, "where are you?"

It is the first question that Adam, the first human, had to confront after he forfeited his authority to dominate the earth in accordance with God's instructions.

'And they heard the voice of the LORD God walking in the garden in the cool of the day: and Adam and his wife hid themselves from the presence of the LORD God amongst the trees of the garden. And the LORD God called unto Adam, and said unto him, "Where are you?"' [1]

"Where are you?" is a question that demands honest self-evaluation and provides a solid foundation for genuine repentance. I don't mean the repentance characterised by shedding a few tears at a church altar and then returning to 'business as usual'. I mean the repentance in which radical change actually occurs because of a transformed mind-set.

Unfortunately, it is a question that many people seek most to avoid, Christians included. Instead, they bury this gnawing question under a mass of religious activity, social engagements, civic programmes or career pursuits.

However, rather than stifle this question, it is important, nay critical, that we each answer this question honestly in order to make necessary adjustments that will move us from where we are right now, to where we really ought to be in our journey towards destiny.

In a marathon race, once you take a wrong turn, no matter how hard you run, failure is the inevitable outcome because you will not arrive at the correct destination. The same is true for real life...

This is why you should regularly take time out to explore your answers to this question or as the wise king put it, *"Ponder the path of your feet, and let all your ways be established."*[2] The question demands that you:

- Understand the purpose for your existence i.e. the assignment for which God caused you to be born.

- Have in place a set of milestones that tell you how far you are in your journey. These are the life goals you develop in the light of your God-ordained purpose. You should also evaluate your progress towards the fulfilment of those goals.

- Identify the reasons why you are where you are e.g. poor choice of friends, career, time usage, or weak relationship with God, etc.

Finally, ensure you make the necessary corrections and follow through with appropriate action to set you back on track, so that you may be able to answer correctly when our King and Lord of all creation asks, "Where are you?"

YOUR DECISIONS... YOUR FUTURE

A wise man once said, "The secret of your future is hidden in your daily routine." This simple statement captures the powerful truth that the decisions you make today will have an impact on the tomorrow you are creating.

You are the sum-total of all the decisions you've made in your yesterdays and your life is the product of your choices. Nothing more, nothing less.

The Bible is an encyclopaedia of decisions made by humans throughout the ages. Over three hundred times in His Word, God says, "**If**" and then outlines the consequences of the decisions we make.

God said to His people, "*Now therefore, **if** you will obey my voice indeed, and keep my covenant, then you shall be a peculiar treasure unto me above all people: for all the earth is mine.*"[3]

He also said, "***If** you are willing and obedient, you shall eat the good of the land. But if you refuse and rebel, you shall be devoured with the sword: for the mouth of the LORD hath spoken it.*"[4]

To put it simply, your future is in your hands...

God desires that you enjoy the best that His Kingdom has to offer spiritually, emotionally, physically, financially and in every area of human existence. However, the extent to which you enjoy these depends on the choices you make.

If you decided to eat hefty portions of high calorie food on a daily basis, do not pretend to be surprised that you are now ten stone heavier than you ought to weigh. The secret of your weight is in your daily helpings of fried food.

If you decided to fill your time daily with negative television programming, do not be surprised that your mind is now filled with images and messages that are perhaps destroying your relationships, stifling your creativity and even nullifying your faith in God's ability to bring you through any difficulties you are facing.

If your daily routine has consistently excluded spending time with The Holy Spirit in the place of prayer and worship, it should be no surprise that you are weighed down by fear, emotional lethargy and spiritual weakness.

Dear friend, make today the beginning of a new daily routine. Decide to start each day in prayer and meditation with The LORD, then discover and pursue His wisdom and assignment for you for that day.

You possess the power of choice. Use it wisely…because your daily decisions are indeed creating your future of tremendous crises or blessings.

LIFE ABUNDANTLY

Jesus Christ made the following proclamation, *"The thief comes only to steal, to kill, and to destroy; I came that they might have life, and have it abundantly."*[5]

Since Jesus says what He means and means what He says, we can safely accept that His promise of abundant life is a promise that cannot fail and no demon from hell or person on earth can overturn His promise of abundant life for you.

However, you can voluntarily or wilfully reject His gift and choose to live below the fullness of life He brought for you and paid for with His own life on the cross of Calvary. Such a choice is made when you choose to live persistently in disobedience to God's commands.

Sin is the quickest and surest way to ensure that you do not partake of the abundant life Jesus brought. It locks you out of God's presence and causes God Himself to pour out His wrath.

The prophet Jeremiah understood the direct connection between sin and its penalties and expressed this in his lamentations for Jerusalem and Judah when they reaped the whirlwind of destruction from the seeds of iniquity they had sown.

He proclaimed, *"The LORD is righteous; for I have rebelled against his commandment: hear, I pray you, all people, and behold my sorrow: my virgins and my young men are gone into captivity,"*[6] and

"He has hedged me about, that I cannot get out: he has made my chain heavy. Also, when I cry and shout, he shuts out my prayer. He has enclosed my ways with hewn stone; he has made my paths crooked."[7]

As the world experiences tremendous pressure from social, moral and environmental disasters, it is an opportune time to reflect on the need for every person on the earth to strive to walk in truth and righteousness.

You simply cannot afford to toy with sin. God demands holiness (integrity of character based on His standards) of every human, and those who yield to His demand will be partakers of the abundant life He promised, not just in the present age but also in eternity.

WHAT HAVE YOU DONE WITH IT?

James the apostle admonishes clearly in the scriptures that the pathway to blessing is in acting upon the truth of God's word that you receive. He penned the following words:

"But you yourselves become doers of the word, and not hearers only deceiving your own selves. For if anyone is a hearer of the word and not a doer, he is like a man who observes his natural face in a mirror; for he observes himself and goes away and immediately forgets what kind of person he was.

But the one who looks intently at the perfect law, that of liberty, and continues in it, not having become a forgetful hearer but a doer of the work, this one shall be blessed in his doing."[8]

The above passage reinforces the idea that God is not particularly impressed by the weekly appearances at Sunday morning services that do not translate into action that positively impacts your home, workplace, business or community.

God has called believers in Christ Jesus to become the salt of the earth, and like salt, we are expected to influence any environment in which we are placed.

This influence however is to be exerted through the quality of excellence displayed in your daily work. Daniel was a captive slave who rose to great prominence in ancient Babylon and the secret of his success is captured by these words:

"Then this Daniel was preferred above the presidents and princes, because an excellent spirit (attitude) was in him; and the king thought to set him over the whole realm."[9]

Daniel's attitude infused every aspect of his daily work in the government to such a degree that even those who hated him had to admit that '*they could find no fault with him concerning his work; forasmuch as he was faithful, neither was there any error or fault found in him."*[10]

The Bible is not a compendium of religious sayings to be used for 'devotions'... It is an intricate collection of principles and precepts that God expects every human to explore, understand and apply to our daily living. This would in turn let *"your light shine before men, so that they may see your good works, and glorify your Father who is in Heaven."*[11]

Always remember... God is more interested in your doing than your hearing. So... "What have you done with all you've heard?"

CHANGING THE WORLD

Listening to the news media and observing what happens even in our local environments gives cause for concern about the state of our world.

However, there is a solution to the myriad problems that earth faces and that solution is expressed in the following words... *"For the earnest expectation of the creation eagerly waits for the revealing of the sons of God."*[12]

In essence, the world needs a certain group of beings to arise from their self-induced stupor, shake off the cobwebs of inferiority and step forward to take their rightful place in the affairs of the earth. These beings, called the sons of God, refer to you! The blood-washed, Holy Spirit-filled citizen of the Kingdom of God sent into the earth for such a time as this.

Jesus the Christ calls you 'the light of the world'[13], implying that where confusion, darkness and ignorance of the right solutions abounds, you are to bring illumination, wisdom and God-inspired solutions.

As followers of Christ, we have responsibility for our world and we can no longer ignore or sidestep that responsibility. You cannot blame the ungodly for making a mess of our communities and our world if you refuse to step out of your four-walled comfort zone (perhaps religious cage) and engage actively in bringing solutions to our world's issues.

Whenever God wants to bring change to a community, His preferred approach is recorded in these words, *"And I sought for a man among them that should make up the hedge, and stand in the gap before me for the land, that I should not destroy it: but I found none."*[14]

God desires that you come into a place of influence in your local, national or international environment so that you can be His mouthpiece to speak His counsel and bring His solutions to the world's problems.

However, you will need to earn the right to be heard, because no one listens to or takes the mediocre seriously. Therefore, mediocrity is no longer an option for you as a follower of Christ.

It is time to break free of average thinking and average living. Discover your latent gifting, refine your God-given abilities, and release them in service excellence to a world that is already waiting in earnest expectation for you to show up.

God wants to change our world and He wants to do it through you!

It's The Process

You had a dream... And you understand without a shadow of doubt that you are destined for greatness... but then those you thought would love you and support you in your quest to reach your dream turn against you and do everything in their power to destroy you... Welcome to the world of Joseph!

You know that God has placed His Hand upon your life and anointed you to become a great leader in your generation... However, those you hoped would recognise and celebrate the grace upon your life have made it their life's mission to ensure that you never fulfil the greatness that is resident within you... Welcome to the world of David!

You have discovered your assignment for your generation and are fully persuaded that you have been ordained to bring hope and deliverance to a people languishing in abject degradation... But those same people you thought would welcome you with open arms, because of the purpose of God upon your life to bring them deliverance, reject you and expose you to potential destruction... Welcome to the world of Moses!

Resting in your heart is the wisdom and counsel flowing from the throne room of God. It positions you for leadership and great exploits... Then you end up as a slave in a foreign land... However, your gifting and God-imparted abilities elevate you to greatness... Yet there are those who are determined to see you fail and are prepared to engineer your downfall in any way possible... Welcome to the world of Daniel!

Dear friend, welcome to the world of Champions!

There is always an initial gap between your dreams of your God-ordained destiny and its fulfilment... It is called 'The Process'.

It is the process that all great Champions must go through in order to test your commitment to the dream and to refine your character.

The process demands perseverance, patience, a teachable spirit and above all a heart of love to see beyond the actions of those who would seek to destroy you.

It also demands that you cultivate the attitude captured by the words of the leader, Paul, as he declared, *"And we know that all things work together for good to them that love God, to them who are the called according to his purpose."*[15]

Don't begrudge the process. It is the price that must be paid for the reward of the greatness that lies within you.

THE HEART OF TRUE LOVE

One of the saddest commentaries on the state of the world today is the violence and destruction that characterises human relationships. Even for Christian churches locally, nationally and globally, the unpleasant truth is that it is riddled with cliques, superficial relationships, denominationalism and outright fragmentation.

The prime test that the King of the Kingdom of God has set for every citizen of His kingdom is the very test that too many are failing. However, not only are they continually failing the test, they are too proud to examine their test results and undergo the necessary changes to enable them pass for the future.

The test question is this:

"Is there anyone in your immediate environment who could benefit from a genuine expression of friendship and love from you but whom you have ignored, neglected or always said the usual, superficial religious greetings to?"

The LORD has made it absolutely clear in the Bible about His expectations of every believer… Break up the cliques and the 'exclusive clubs' and extend love to every human on this planet, not just those who meet the qualifications to join your religious club. He expressed it this way…

"You have heard that it was said: 'You shall love your neighbor and hate your enemy.' But I say to you, love your enemies, and pray for those who persecute you, so that you may be sons of your Father in Heaven, because He causes His sun to rise on the evil and the good, and sends rain on the righteous and the unrighteous.

For if you love those who love you, what reward do you have? Do not the tax collectors do the same? And if you greet your brethren only, what do you do more? Do not even the tax collectors do the same? Be ye therefore perfect, even as your Father which is in heaven is perfect."[16]

The true measure of your relationship with Christ is not in the religious demonstrations and rituals observed every Sunday... It is in the genuine, daily, practical expressions of warmth and friendship borne out of a heart of true love for all people.

As John, one of the early church leaders said, "*If anyone says, 'I love God,' and hates his brother, he is a liar; for he who does not love his brother whom he has seen does not have the power to love God whom he has not seen.*"[17]

Love is the litmus test of true discipleship... No more, no less!

Each Day in His Presence

What is it that God, the ultimate King, the creator of the universe desires the most from human beings, the crowning glory of His creative efforts? What is it that He looks for when He looks over the balustrades of heavenly glory at His creation below?

He is seeking for true worshippers... a new breed of humanity that delights in His presence and is willing to lay aside all pretension and religiousness. He is seeking for those who truly hunger, not for what you can get out of Him, but for Him.

Jesus, the Christ, expressed this ardent desire of the Godhead in the following words, *"But an hour is coming, and now is, when the true worshippers will worship the Father in spirit and truth; for such the Father seeks to worship Him."*[18]

God is not impressed with the religious shows and weekly rituals of singing and dancing and activities that many people call worship. He is looking past all of that into the hearts of all of us who come before Him, to see whether we have the heart of David.

His search is for a heart that lives by the words, *"A day in your courts is better than a thousand. I would rather be a doorkeeper in the house of my God, than to dwell in the tents of wickedness."*[19]

God desires for us to live each day in the glow of His holy presence.

The many things that people pursue only bring transient pleasure but... Oh for the glory of His enduring presence ...

David the king understood this when he proclaimed, *"You will show me the path of life: in your presence is fullness of joy; at your right hand there are pleasures for evermore."*[20]

Paul, the Apostle, also recognised that, "*Now the Lord is that Spirit: and where the Spirit of the Lord is, there is liberty.*"[21]

Remember this however; God will not release His manifest glory frivolously! He admonishes us through His prophet, "*And you shall seek me, and find me, when you shall search for me with all your heart.*"[22]

My fervent hope is this… that all humans, and more especially those who are called by His name, will truly crave to spend each day in His presence, and like Moses (see Exodus 34: 29), transform our world by the glory and the glow of His presence radiating out of our lives.

REST IN PRAISE

Dear Friend, what do you do when it seems like your world is falling apart? How do you respond when it looks like everywhere that you turn, there's a crisis awaiting your attention?

How do you handle life, when you feel you've tried everything you know how and yet nothing seems to be working?

Perhaps your current circumstances make you feel financially, emotionally, physically or spiritually drained and it seems your life's vehicle is running on an empty tank.

Well friend, at such a time as this, the most effective course of action is to R.I.P.

Don't you worry… it is time to Rest in Praise!

Paul, the Apostle, found himself in such a situation where everything seemed out of control. He was thrown into jail, at the mercy of the Roman authorities, seemingly facing the premature termination of his life… and yet, along with his ministry partner, Silas, he chose to enter into the sanctuary of praise.

Instead of worrying and fretting about his adverse circumstances, he chose to rest in praise. He understood that true praise translates you into the realm of the supernatural, which causes the Kingdom of God to work and perform the impossible on your behalf.

The Bible records that, "*At midnight Paul and Silas prayed, and **sang praises unto God**: and the prisoners heard them. And suddenly there was a great earthquake, so that the foundations of the prison were shaken: and immediately all the doors were opened, and every one's bands were loosed.*"[23]

Jehoshaphat, a king in ancient Israel, faced what might be considered insurmountable odds. Three nations, mighty in battle and determined to destroy Israel, had arrayed themselves in battle, expecting to fulfill their wicked schemes against the people of God.

But through the wisdom of God, Jehoshaphat *"appointed singers unto the LORD, and that should praise the beauty of holiness, as they went out before the army, and to say, Praise the LORD; for his mercy endures for ever. And when they began to sing and to praise, the LORD set ambushes against the children of Ammon, Moab, and mount Seir, which were come against Judah; and they were destroyed."*[24]

Friend, despite what your enemies may think... it's not over until you win. The weapon of praise is still available to you today. Reach deep into your spirit and allow songs of praise to our living God to stream out of your being.

As you do, the LORD of hosts who delights in the praises of His people (see Psalm 22:3) will step into the midst of your praise and show Himself strong on your behalf.

STILL STANDING

To all saints who may be going through a rough patch, there is a promise from the Eternal King that guarantees that you must and will overcome. This promise is recorded through His prophet in the following words…

"The righteous shall flourish like the palm tree: he shall grow like a cedar in Lebanon.

Those that be planted in the house of the LORD shall flourish in the courts of our God.

They shall still bring forth fruit in old age; they shall be fat and flourishing; to show that the LORD is upright: he is my rock, and there is no unrighteousness in him."[25]

One of the key qualities of a healthy palm tree is its ability to withstand extreme weather conditions, including snow blizzards and even winds of hurricane force.

As a believer in Christ Jesus, within you lies the spirit of endurance and the ability to withstand all that life may throw at you.

Like the palm tree, you may sometimes feel that the winds of adversity are about to blow you over, but be assured of this… because you are solidly planted in the Kingdom of God… you may bend, **but you will not break!**

Another key quality of the palm tree is longevity and fruitfulness even into old age. This is God's expectation for you as He indicates… *"For I know the thoughts that I think toward you, says the LORD, thoughts of peace, and not of evil, to give you an expected end."*[26]

God's desire is for you to continually flourish in the arena of life that He has called you to, even into old age. He is always keen to prosper you in such a way that all those who look upon your life would have to acknowledge that you serve the mighty God who is righteous because He fulfills His promises.

There is, however, a condition necessary for the continued flourishing of a palm tree; regardless of the external weather conditions, internally, its roots must remain in contact with a source of water.

This principle also holds true for you dear friend. You must remain close to the Holy Spirit, your source of living water, in prayer and worship.

As you choose to remain in close contact with the refreshing presence and power of the Holy Spirit, the blizzards of life may blow through, but when it's all over… YOU will be still standing and standing strong.

FOR SUCH A TIME AS THIS

The Bible records the story of a young queen of Persia (ancient Iran) whose exploits are remembered throughout the rest of human history because she responded to the responsibility of a divine mandate to protect her people from destruction.

That young queen, named Esther, fulfilled her assignment because she came to the conclusion that, if it was necessary, she was willing to lay down her life to achieve her mandate. She uttered those immortal words, "*If I perish, I perish*" (see Esther 4: 16) as she recognised that she had come to her position of influence in the Persian kingdom in order to accomplish God's purposes.

Her example illustrates the principle Christ taught us in the following words, "*If any man will come after me, let him deny himself, and take up his cross, and follow me. For whosoever will save his life shall lose it: and whosoever will lose his life for my sake shall find it.*"[27]

Once again, the clarion call is going out to a new generation of saints who will choose to walk in the footsteps of Esther. A people who understand that, "you are come to the kingdom for such a time as this."[28]

God has placed you in your arena of influence for such a time as this so that you can fulfil His divine assignment.

Like Esther, fulfilling your kingdom mandate requires that you carefully evaluate your choices and answer this vital question… are you willing to lay down all that you hold dear, even your life, in order to protect, preserve and fulfil God's purposes?

When called upon to defend Biblical truth in all its ramifications, will you dodge this responsibility in favour of political correctness or will you stand up to be counted for truth in the face of opposition?

That is the choice facing each one of us as citizens of the Kingdom of God. However, as you make the right choices, remember that your strength is not in your own abilities. Like Esther, you need to enter into a greater dimension of God's anointing through the pursuit of His presence in prayer, fasting and a lifestyle of worship.

As God enriches you with His anointing, may your life increasingly radiate His love, peace, wisdom and glory, and dispel every iota of darkness wherever He places you.

A Heart Set on God

With so much political uncertainty, economic upheavals, relationship crises and religious turmoil all around us, it is absolutely critical for everyone of us to heed the injunctions of the wise King Solomon in which he stated, *"Keep your heart with all diligence; for out of it are the issues of life."*[29]

Perhaps you are one of those who are being bombarded by adverse circumstances. Perhaps people around you are using hurtful words or deeds against you in order to satisfy their own warped emotional needs. Or perhaps your work or business situation is in something of a crisis.

Daily living is so turbulent for many that they live in a state of continuous internal turmoil. Their hearts are continually troubled, resulting in a high state of emotional tension or physical stress.

The biblical prescription for dealing with this kind of pressure is found in the words of the ancient prophet:

"You will keep him in perfect peace, whose mind is stayed on you: because he trusts in You."[30]

Dear friend, keep your heart focused on God. Regardless of what is happening externally, keep your internal balance by ensuring your mind stays on God.

The way to accomplish this is to return to the 'quiet and secret place of God's presence.' Spend more time studying the Scriptures. Spend more time knowing the heart of God. Spend more time in quiet contemplation of His majesty and ultimate control over the universe.

As you do so, the Holy Spirit will set you free from the depths of despair and depression that circumstances want to drag you into. The Lord will fill your heart with His peace and restore to you the joy of salvation.

Always remember, every trial is temporary and behind every dark cloud is a silver lining. Or as the Apostle put it, *"For the momentary light matter of our tribulation is working out for us an eternal weight of glory beyond all comparison, we do not contemplate the things which are seen, but at the things which are not seen; for the things which are seen are temporal, but the things which are not seen are eternal."*[31]

Friend, keep your heart stayed on God *"for thus says the Lord GOD, the Holy One of Israel; in returning and rest shall you be saved; in quietness and in confidence shall be your strength…"*[32]

TRUTH... THE KEY TO FREEDOM

Real and sustained progress or success is impossible until you confront truth. The significance of this idea is demonstrated in the lives of many people whose lives are stuck somewhere between mediocrity and bare existence.

Such people are unwilling to face the truth about themselves and consequently end up in a prison of their own making. Unfortunately, many Christians are victims of this self-imposed mental and spiritual blockade that deprives them of living the abundant life that Jesus, the Christ died on the cross of Calvary to purchase for us.

The unwillingness to face truth is often masked by false humility or the desire to hold God responsible for things for which He has already committed into your hands.

The notion that a follower of Christ Jesus can be in bondage is adequately captured in the following passage in scripture: '*Then said Jesus to those Jews who believed on him, "If you continue in my word, then are you my disciples indeed; and you shall know the truth, and the truth shall make you free"*'[33]

In essence, we must continually expose our actions and our results to the light of Biblical truth, and the outcome of this self-evaluation must positively affect our future actions. For example, if you find yourself regularly beset by feelings of jealousy, envy, anger or other negative emotions.... face the truth about yourself.

Blaming your feelings or attitudes on the actions of others only keeps you in bondage. Until you acknowledge the truth and then commit to making the necessary changes with the LORD's help, you cannot experience total freedom.

The Apostle James reinforces the need for us to continually face truth in these words:

"But you yourselves become doers of the word, and not merely hearers who falsely reason with themselves. For if anyone is a hearer of the word and not a doer, he is like a man who observes his natural face in a mirror; for he observes himself and goes away and immediately forgets what kind of person he was.

But the one who looks intently at the perfect law, that of liberty, and continues in it, not having become a forgetful hearer but a doer of work, this one shall be blessed in his doing."[34]

Are there areas of your personal life, your business, your ministry, your work, etc, that are hindering your progress and where change is required? Don't blame God for not making the change for which He has made you responsible.

You know the truth... Do it... Make the change and experience the fullness of freedom to accomplish all that God has called you to accomplish in this generation.

WISDOM...

Almost every problem you and I face is a wisdom problem. But until you recognise and appropriate this simple truth, life remains an exercise in frustration.

If you have marriage problems, financial challenges, health issues, whatever the nature of the problem you face, it can be traced back ultimately to a lack of wisdom in that particular area of life.

How do we know this is true? Because God Himself says so!

He inspired Solomon, the ancient sage of Israel to pen these words:

"Wisdom is the principal thing; therefore, get wisdom: and with all your getting get understanding. Exalt her, and she shall promote you: she shall bring you to honour, when you embrace her. She shall give to your head an ornament of grace: a crown of glory shall she deliver to you.

Hear, O my son, and receive my sayings; and the years of your life shall be many. I have taught you in the way of wisdom; I have led you in right paths. When you go, your steps shall not be straitened; and when you run, you shall not stumble."[35]

Wisdom is the application of God's time-tested, eternally-enduring principles to life's situations. As Solomon, the wise king, also said, *"The thing that has been, it is that which shall be; and that which is done is that which shall be done: and there is no new thing under the sun."*[36]

In essence, everything you currently face, have faced or will face has happened to someone else before, and it already has a solution prescribed in the Bible, God's Word. You simply need to seek for it and you shall find the answer.

God reinforced this principle through His prophet, *"my people are destroyed for lack of knowledge."*[37]

Notice that God did not say that His people are destroyed because of the devil, because of demons or because of any other type of enemy. Rather, ignorance of God's purposes, His desires for you, His success principles and His creative solutions to your challenges, results in destruction.

So, let your heart delight in wisdom; pursue it ardently and be equipped to triumph in all aspects of your life and fulfil your divine assignment to this generation.

THE POWER OF ONE...

One of the fundamental truths that govern creation is that God, the creator, is the God of purpose. And because of this inherent nature, everything He created was and is for a purpose.

He created the sun to bring illumination and warmth to the earth. He created the moon and stars to provide light in the night.

Where the purpose for a thing is not known, there exists tremendous potential for abuse and misuse. Ignorance of the purpose of a thing, however, does not cancel its purpose. It merely limits your ability to maximize the potential of that thing.

For example, if I come across a knife for the first time, there is a great risk that I could use it in ways that would cause injury to me or to others. What about ignorance of the purpose of a bicycle? This may cause me to put it on my shoulders and walk 20 miles to my destination instead of riding the bicycle and making my journey easier and quicker.

In very much the same way, God created you for a purpose... a purpose that you must discover, pursue and fulfill otherwise life becomes an exercise in futility.

David, the beloved king of Israel expressed the truth about purposeful existence in the following words:

"I praise you because I am fearfully and wonderfully made; your works are wonderful, I know that full well. My frame was not hidden from you when I was made in the secret place.

When I was woven together in the depths of the earth, your eyes saw my unformed body. All the days ordained for me were written in your book before one of them came to be."[38]

When God wants to change or deliver a community, a nation, or the even the entire world, He causes one person to be born to fulfill that assignment.

When He wanted to deliver Israel from Egyptian captivity, He caused Moses to be born. When He wanted to save the Jews from destruction in ancient Persia, He caused Esther to be born and to become queen.

When He wanted to save the world from the power of the devil, God did not send an army, He sent one, Jesus the Christ.

God wanted to bring change to your neighbourhood, your city, your nation, your generation... He caused one person to be born... You!

Your assignment is crucial to our generation. That is the power of One.

LET EVERYTHING THAT HAS BREATH…

One of the quickest ways to cut off the flow of favour in a person's life is to develop a heart of ingratitude. Ingratitude shuts off blessings, limits a person's effectiveness in relationships and brings the disfavour of God.

God's perspective on ingratitude is revealed in the following Biblical record:

'Now on his way to Jerusalem, Jesus travelled along the border between Samaria and Galilee. As he was going into a village, ten men who had leprosy met him. They stood at a distance and called out in a loud voice, "Jesus, Master, have pity on us!"

When he saw them, he said, "Go, show yourselves to the priests." And as they went, they were cleansed. One of them, when he saw he was healed, came back, praising God in a loud voice. He threw himself at Jesus' feet and thanked him… and he was a Samaritan.

Jesus asked, "Were not all ten cleansed? Where are the other nine? Was no one found to return and give praise to God except this foreigner?" Then he said to him, "Rise and go; your faith has made you well."'[39]

Evidently, Jesus was not impressed with the other nine who did not return to thank him.

Ingratitude is an attitude that reflects ungodly self-importance and refuses to acknowledge the grace and goodness extended towards us by God and by other people.

It is usually the first sign of a life filled with pride. And God Himself absolutely detests pride as He said, *"Whoever secretly slanders his neighbour, him I will destroy; the one who has a haughty look and a proud heart, him I will not endure."*[40]

The psalmist understood that God deserves all praise, glory and honour from every living creature and therefore proclaimed, *"Let everything that has breath praise the LORD. Praise the LORD."*[41]

If you are breathing right now... you are qualified to praise God. The fact that you are still breathing means that your assignment on earth is not yet completed and you are a potential candidate for divine favour.

Let your heart soar on the wings of praise today. The heart of gratitude will lift you above the dark clouds of life's situations to see the sun of God's grace, power and mercy waiting to break through and transform your life.

You are alive, you have His breath... Praise The LORD.

RIGHTEOUSNESS – THE PRIORITY

Events in the USA once again bring into sharp focus the need for every follower of Christ to live by the following injunction from Paul, the Apostle:

"So then, my beloved, even as you have always obeyed, not as in my presence only, but now much more in my absence, work out your own salvation with fear and trembling."[42]

The fall from grace of a national Christian leader, overseeing a body representing 30 million Christians in the USA, severely affected many believers and provided ammunition for many critics and opponents of the body of Christ.

However, such events should serve to remind us that every leader is human and as citizens of the kingdom of God, now more than ever is the time to intensify our prayers for Christian leaders and leaders of our nations who are in the forefront of warfare against the kingdom of darkness.

Furthermore, rather than sitting in judgement over your brother or sister who has fallen short of the mark of moral excellence, use the time for personal introspection and re-evaluation of your relationship with Christ our King and His Kingdom.

It is a time for us to ask ourselves the question… What really is my priority in life?

Jesus established the core priority for every human when He proclaimed, *"… seek first the kingdom of God and His righteousness…"*[43]

According to the King, your key priority in life should not be the pursuit of career, or church recognition, or social mobility or material things. It should be the pursuit of His kingdom (which is the governing influence of God in your life and your world) and His righteousness (which is the proper alignment with His will, purpose and instructions).

The ardent, daily pursuit of the kingdom of God and His righteousness leaves no room for other things contrary to His will.

Dear Friend, the Kingdom of Heaven is forcefully advancing, despite all attempts by human and satanic forces to obstruct its progress. As we pray for the restoration and healing of the wounded soldiers, my earnest prayer for you is that, you will continually place first things first.

As you pursue the righteousness of God, may you shine as a city set on a hill, which cannot be hidden, reminding a sceptical world that there is still a body of people committed to living in integrity, truth, righteous justice, godly wisdom, peace and love on earth... All of which are components of the Kingdom of our God and of His Christ.

BACK TO BASICS

One of the greatest challenges facing humanity today is the unending pursuit of self-interest to the detriment of others.

This trait is manifested by corporate executives driven by greed to defraud their companies, by leaders bent on preventing their followers from maximising their potential, and by many people hell-bent on illicit pleasures, fuelled by immorality, drugs, alcohol, violence or other vices, without thought for the consequences of their choices on other people.

In essence, many people are living lives devoid of true love.

Regrettably, this attitude of self-centredness and lack of genuine love has crept into the church, such that the lives of many Christians can be accurately described in the following words... *"These people draw near to Me with their mouth, and honour Me with their lips, but their heart is far from Me. And in vain they worship Me, teaching as doctrines the commandments of men."*[44]

It is important, once again, for every believer in Christ to go back to basics and search our hearts as we ponder this question... "What is the most important principle for effective living in the kingdom of God?"

Over two thousand years ago, a religious leader sought the answer to this question and in response, 'Jesus said to him, *"You shall love the LORD your God with all your heart, with all your soul, and with all your mind." This is the first and great commandment. And the second is like it: You shall love your neighbour as yourself. On these two commandments hang all the Law and the Prophets."*'[45]

God, however, does not leave His definition of love to our imaginations. He clearly expressed His kind of love in the following words:

"Love suffers long and is kind; love does not envy; love does not parade itself, is not puffed up; does not behave rudely, does not seek its own, is not provoked, thinks no evil; does not rejoice in iniquity, but rejoices in the truth; bears all things, believes all things, hopes all things, endures all things. Love never fails..."[46]

Dear friend, Jesus stated that we are the 'salt of the earth',[47] meaning that we possess the ability and the responsibility to influence earth positively.

If we all went back to the basics of genuine love, our homes, our churches, our jobs, our communities and our nations would be that much better.

THE CELEBRATION OF INTEGRITY

Whenever we celebrate the birth of Christ Jesus, during the Christmas season, regardless of the arguments about the actual historical date of Christ's birth, what is important to note is that, it is a celebration of integrity... God's integrity.

About 700 years before the first Christmas, God spoke through one of His prophets the following words, *"For unto us a Child is born, unto us a Son is given; and the government will be upon His shoulder. And His name will be called Wonderful, Counsellor, Mighty God, Everlasting Father, Prince of Peace.*

Of the increase of His government and peace there will be no end, upon the throne of David and over His kingdom, to order it and establish it with judgment and justice from that time forward, even forever. The zeal of the Lord of hosts will perform this."[48]

In this prophecy, God promised mankind that He would be restoring a government to the earth. He did not promise to send a religion filled with rites and ritualistic programmes that we now call Christianity. The Almighty promised us that He would be sending us a Kingdom that would be characterised by the unique nature of its King.

The birth of Jesus, the Christ heralded the arrival of the eternal King, a fact celebrated by creation (the bright star) and the wise men of ancient times as recorded thus:

'Now after Jesus was born in Bethlehem of Judea in the days of Herod the king, behold, wise men from the East came to Jerusalem, saying, "Where is He who has been born King of the Jews? For we have seen His star in the East and have come to worship Him."'[49]

Christ's birth also heralded the return of the Kingdom of God, characterised by peace, justice, wise counsel, might (or power), wonder, eternal sustenance, all of which are products of the unique nature of Jesus, our King.

We celebrate Christmas because the zeal of the Lord of Hosts performed that which He promised.

Dear friend, Christmas is a reminder that you can rest, secure in the knowledge that the integrity of God remains sure and steadfast, unto eternity.

If you do not yet belong to the Kingdom of God, now is the time to cross over. Receive Christ as King and Lord (owner) of your life and step into the marvellous benefits of citizenship in an eternal Kingdom filled with righteousness, peace and joy.

Just as the Kingdom returned, according to God's plan and promises, His promises to every citizen of His Kingdom will be fulfilled according to His divine plan.

As the bells jingle and we proclaim, Merry Christmas, may each Christmas moment, and every day thereafter, remind you of God's integrity and inspire you to live like your King... with the utmost integrity.

REACHING FORWARD

Dear friend, warmest congratulations! You made it this far, despite all the challenges that life has thrown at you this year; you survived and have arrived at the threshold of a new season of your life.

In some respects, you are like Joshua and the children of Israel as they arrived at the borders of the land God promised to them. They looked over the waters of Jordan to behold a land filled with goodness, blessings and, most importantly, the land that would be the fulfilment of God's purposes for their generation and the future of humanity.

Similarly, you may be standing on the threshold of another season of life, poised to enter new territory and accomplish the next phase of God's purpose for your life and your generation.

The words that the Almighty spoke to Joshua at that critical moment of transition are just as applicable to you today…

"… Now then, you and all these people, get ready to cross the Jordan River into the land I am about to give to them. I will give you every place where you set your foot, as I promised Moses… No one will be able to stand up against you all the days of your life. As I was with Moses, so I will be with you; I will never leave you nor forsake you.

Be strong and courageous, because you will lead these people to inherit the land I swore to their forefathers to give them. Be strong and very courageous. Be careful to obey all the law my servant Moses gave you; do not turn from it to the right or to the left, that you may be successful wherever you go. Do not let this Book of the Law depart from your mouth; meditate on it day and night, so that you may be careful to do everything written in it. Then you will be prosperous and successful.

Have I not commanded you? Be strong and courageous. Do not be terrified; do not be discouraged, for the LORD your God will be with you wherever you go."[50]

Three times, God highlighted a key mental and spiritual disposition you will require in order to take all the territory He has earmarked for you in your next season... Courage!

Friend, as you cross over into this coming phase, let your heart also resound with the power of God's words... Be strong and very courageous... Then reach forward in the knowledge that this is your moment to achieve greatness with your life for the Kingdom of God.

FAITHFUL

As your journey into your year progresses, Paul the Apostle, in the following words, expresses one of the fundamental truths that must remain close to our hearts:

"Being confident of this very thing, that he which has begun a good work in you will perform it until the day of Jesus Christ."[51]

Each season of life comes with its own fair share of obstacles and victories, tears and joys but in all of these things, remember that you began through God's grace and He has promised, *"…I will never leave you, nor forsake you, so that we may boldly say, The Lord is my helper, and I will not fear what man shall do unto me."*[52]

Each step of the way will be a faith walk with God, knowing that He who was with you in the beginning will also be with you in the end because He is the Alpha and the Omega (see Revelation 22: 13).

Friend, this is a time to define and refine your vision… a time to discover or recover your sense of divine purpose… a time to live in the fullest understanding of the truth that, *"we are his workmanship, created in Christ Jesus unto good works, which God had before ordained that we should walk in them."*[53]

And because you are His workmanship, your success in the coming days will be measured, not by how much money you make, material goods you acquire, social ladders you climb or religious accolades you receive; true success will be measured by how much you accomplished the 'good works' that God ordained for you to accomplish even before you were born.

In essence, define your success by the discovery, pursuit and fulfillment of your divine purpose.

The LORD, who gave you your assignment, is faithful to bring it to pass. However, He desires willing participants in the fulfillment of His plans for humanity. He desires a people walking in the divine original mandate and nature, "*let us make man in our image, after our likeness...*"[54]

The original nature of God includes faithfulness... that is His expectation of you, His offspring... faithfulness to your God-assigned purpose and to being the best you can possibly be in your service to God and His creation; humanity.

THE SECRET INGREDIENT

You probably have an aunt, parent or other relative who is the family expert in cooking a special dish. The kind of dish that makes you wiggle your toes in delight when you eat it.

Everyone who is familiar with the intricacies of exceptional cooking understands that those dishes demand a special ingredient (often kept secret), which makes the dish special. Without that ingredient, the meal would simply taste ordinary.

In very much the same way, there is a special ingredient necessary to transform the life of every Christian believer from religious mediocrity to exceptional effectiveness in the Kingdom of God. That simple ingredient is revealed in the words of Apostle Paul, "*Follow peace with all men, and holiness, without which no man shall see the Lord.*"[55]

Too many Christians have been misled into believing the lie that religious, church-based performance that earns the praises of men is the measure of spiritual success. Nothing could be further from the truth.

As the apostle stated, no one can '**see**' (which means experience, partake of and live in) the LORD without holiness.

But how do you attain holiness? The answer is partly found in the Biblical injunctions:

- "*Having therefore these promises, dearly beloved, let us cleanse ourselves from all filthiness of the flesh and spirit, perfecting holiness in the (reverential) fear of God.*"[56]

- "*Who shall not fear you, O Lord, and glorify your name for you alone are holy.*"[57]

God alone is holy and is the source and sustainer of holiness.

Holiness is therefore a by-product of walking in intimacy with the Holy One. This in turn requires a commitment to live by His standards of right or wrong.

Such intimacy is a 24/7 proposition, refined and reinforced by a life of ceaseless prayer and the pursuit of righteousness. As Paul put it, *"Just as you used to offer the parts of your body as servants to impurity and to ever-increasing wickedness, so now offer them as servants to righteousness leading to holiness."*[58]

Holiness, underpinned by a vibrant prayer life, is the gateway to spiritual power and the abundant life Christ promised.

Friend, choose today to add that secret ingredient to your life.

Winning the Battle of the Mind

There is an old African proverb that states, "If the enemy within does not kill us, the enemy without can do us no harm."

This simple, yet profound statement, captures the essence of the battle that each and every one of us must win, each and every day.

It has often been said that the mind is the battlefield upon which great victories are won or lost... a truth that permeates the Biblical records of human existence.

Satan's attack against Adam and Eve in the Garden of Eden (see Genesis 3) was an attack against their mind. His attack against Jesus, the Christ, in the wilderness of Judea (see Matthew 4) was not with shield and spear, it was a battle against Jesus' mind, designed to bring Him into doubt about His self-identity.

The battle for the mind is intensifying with Satan deploying an increasing array of tools such as corrupt content on television, radio, internet, books and other types of media, against the pursuit of a pure heart or wholesome mind.

Understanding this truth must inevitably lead us to heed the words of the wise king, "*Guard your heart (your mind) with all diligence, for out of it spring the issues of life.*"[59]

Jesus stated in the following words, that good or evil is the product of the human mind... "*A good man out of the good treasure of his heart brings forth good; and an evil man out of the evil treasure of his heart brings forth evil; For out of the abundance of the heart his mouth speaks.*"[60]

Remember that the words you speak frame or create your world.

So... if you desire to win the battle of the mind, what weapons are effective in your quest for victory?

The most important is the commitment to intensified study and meditation on the principles and precepts of God's word...The Bible.

Not the passive, daily ten-minute or once-a-week dip into the Scriptures to fulfil your religious quota, but a passionate quest to fill your mind to overflowing abundance with life-enhancing truth.

As you spend more time studying the Scriptures, you will find that your mind is filled with godly wisdom, and fortified against ideas that militate against your success.

Therein lies the most potent key to winning the battle of the mind.

Citizenship Rights

One crucial truth that every follower of Jesus Christ must understand is that His prime purpose is the restoration of the kingdom of God on earth and not the formation of a religious club called Christianity.

The power of this difference is rooted in the fact that whilst most Christians live as religious creatures, *a true believer is a legal being with rights of citizenship.*

The Bible states, "*...our citizenship is in heaven, from which we also eagerly wait for the Saviour, the Lord Jesus Christ, who will transform our lowly body that it may be conformed to His glorious body, according to the working by which He is able even to subdue all things to Himself.*"[61]

Understanding that you are a citizen of a kingdom... indeed the most powerful Kingdom in the universe... gives you a sense of holy confidence and protects you from being intimidated or wilfully abused by humans or by demonic spirits.

The power of citizenship is demonstrated in the experience of Paul the Apostle in the following passage:

'*As they stretched him out to flog him, Paul said to the centurion standing there, "Is it legal for you to flog a Roman citizen who hasn't even been found guilty?" When the centurion heard this, he went to the commander and reported it. "What are you going to do?" he asked. "This man is a Roman citizen."*

The commander went to Paul and asked, "Tell me, are you a Roman citizen?"

"Yes, I am," he answered. Then the commander said, "I had to pay a big price for my citizenship." "But I was born a citizen," Paul replied.

Those who were about to question him withdrew immediately. The commander himself was alarmed when he realised that he had put Paul, a Roman citizen, in chains."[62]

By invoking his rights as a Roman citizen, Paul was protected from the evil plans of his enemies. Similarly, when you understand your rights as a citizen of the Kingdom of God, you are able to boldly confront and overcome the plans of your adversaries.

As citizens of God's Kingdom, Christ our King confers on us benefits and privileges such as Divine health (see James 5: 14 – 15; Mark 7: 27), Provision (Matthew 6: 31 – 32), Wisdom and Spiritual insight (Matthew 13: 11), Protection (Psalm 91: 11 – 12) and many more.

Your responsibility is to know your constitutional rights (Biblical truth), remain rightly aligned with the government of heaven (righteousness) and invoke your citizenship rights when circumstances demand, being confident that your heavenly government will fulfil its responsibilities towards you as a citizen in good standing.

Transformed

When you look in a mirror, what do you see?

Someone might possibly say, "what a silly question, of course I see my face". And that response would seem right to you. But perhaps there ought to be a different response...

The apostle Paul, speaking by the inspiration of the Holy Spirit, wrote:

"But we all with our face having been unveiled, reflecting as in a mirror the glory of the Lord, are being transformed into the same image from glory to glory, just as from the Lord, the Spirit."[63]

Paul was reiterating a truth that often eludes many Christians, and yet this truth is the central message of the Bible, right from the creation in Genesis.

The truth is this... when you look into the mirror, you are looking at the Glory of God.

Or you ought to be looking at His glory... and this image of Christ's glory should lay the foundation for the daily process of transformation in your life.

God's 'glory' refers to His nature, His essence, His character, His very being. That is what God deposited in every human on the face of the earth. This nature remains dormant until you receive Jesus Christ as Saviour and King, and then comes alive as His Holy Spirit returns into your life.

Paul put it this way, *"for the love of Christ constrains us; because we thus judge, that if one died for all, then were all dead: And that he died for all, that they which live should not henceforth live unto themselves, but unto him which died for them, and rose again.*

Wherefore henceforth we know no man according to the flesh: yes, though we have known Christ according to the flesh, yet now henceforth we no longer know him so.

Therefore if any man be in Christ, he is a new creature: old things are passed away; behold all things are become new."[64]

Dear friend, each day is an opportunity to examine yourself in the mirror of God's word and then seek the help of the Holy Spirit to engage in the process of change that moves you from your present level to a higher level of love, peace, joy, righteousness, productivity, justice, holiness, patience… all the things that are the nature of God whose Spirit dwells in you.

At the end of each day, it is crucial to be able to look in that mirror again and say with certainty… "Today, in this aspect of my life, I have been transformed."

LET IT SHINE

God's word states, "*the spirit of man is the candle of the LORD, searching all the inward parts of the belly*"[65] and describes Jesus Christ as "*the true light who gives light to every person who comes into the world...*"[66]

These statements imply that God has deposited within you a light that shines like no other. His light in you is unique in its brightness and in its effect upon the landscape of creation. That light is a piece of Himself that God has chosen to send into the world for such a time as this.

However, the greatest challenge most of us face is revealed in the following words of The Master; "*You are the light of the world. A city on a hill cannot be hidden. Neither do people light a lamp and put it under a bowl. Instead they put it on its stand, and it gives light to everyone in the house. In the same way, let your light shine before men, that they may see your good deeds and glorify your Father in heaven.*"[67]

The circumstances of life, negative actions of your fellow humans and worst of all the inner voice of doubt and fear all seem to be focussed on one thing... destroying the light within you or ensuring that it never shines bright enough for the world to see.

So how do you respond to these influences and how do you break free of their hold upon the manifestation of your destiny?

Simply put... Prepare for War!

Jesus said, "*And from the days of John the Baptist until now the kingdom of heaven suffers violence, and the violent take it by force.*"[68]

As a citizen of the Kingdom of God, you must be willing to engage the enemies of your purpose in spiritual warfare through the power of intense prayer and the tenacious pursuit of God's wisdom to excel in your area of gifting. The world needs what you have to offer… that is why God caused you to be born.

Indeed, His word announces clearly that, *"the creation waits in eager expectation for the sons of God to be revealed. For the creation was subjected to frustration, not by its own choice, but by the will of the one who subjected it, in hope that the creation itself will be liberated from its bondage to decay and brought into the glorious freedom of the children of God."*[69]

You have a responsibility towards God and towards the rest of His creation to manifest His purpose deposited within you. Our generation needs to see the light that you are carrying within you… Let it shine!

HEARING THE VOICE OF GOD

Nowadays, one of the most difficult things for many people to accomplish is quietness in their daily living environment. Noises of different sorts, from vehicles, neighbours, televisions, radios, family members and from many other sources all compete for our attention.

Consequently, it is becoming almost impossible for many Christians to clearly discern the voice of God, resulting in the tragedy that regularly manifests itself in the common, but misguided statement, "The LORD told me to........" However, the outcomes of these so-called instructions from God are often negligible at best and catastrophic at worst.

Yet, clear discernment of His voice is a prime key to effective living and fulfilling Christ's will for our lives on a daily basis.

The prophet Elijah had the following encounter with God that emphasises the crucial benefits of quietness:

"The LORD said, Go out and stand on the mountain in the presence of the LORD, for the LORD is about to pass by. Then a great and powerful wind tore the mountains apart and shattered the rocks before the LORD, but the LORD was not in the wind. After the wind there was an earthquake, but the LORD was not in the earthquake.

After the earthquake came a fire but the LORD was not in the fire. And after the fire came a gentle whisper. When Elijah heard it, he pulled his cloak over his face and went out and stood at the mouth of the cave. Then a voice said to him, "What are you doing here, Elijah?"[70]

Notice that the voice of God came, not as a loud shout, but as a quiet whisper. But because Elijah was in an environment and attitude of stillness, he could discern it.

Jesus often withdrew from the noise of His environment to spend time in quietness in the presence of His Heavenly Father and always returned re-invigorated in the power of the Holy Spirit to fulfil His Father's commission for the day.

This is the pattern that we each must cultivate in order to live focussed, effective lives. God's word states, *"For thus says the Lord GOD, the Holy One of Israel; in returning and rest shall you be saved; in quietness and in confidence shall be your strength: but you would not."*[71]

Nothing better equips you to achieve victory in the fulfilment of your God-ordained purpose than the ability to clearly hear God's voice.

Find a secret place of prayer, a place and time of quietness where you can daily enjoy meditative study of God's word and intimate communion with your Heavenly Father… and your life will be refreshed with the peace, love and sense of purpose that comes from clearly hearing His voice. This in turn, positions you to effectively fulfil your divine assignment for every day in your job, business or other worthy endeavours.

YOUR THOUGHTS... SHAPE YOUR WORLD

One of the most popular quotes with Christians is, "*As a man thinks in his heart, so is he.*" This saying is drawn from Proverbs 23: 7 and captures one of the most powerful, yet ignored, truths about human existence.

When truly understood, this simple quote places the responsibility for your life squarely in your hands. In essence, if you are spiritually, financially or physically impoverished, the only person to blame is yourself. Which perhaps explains why everywhere Jesus went, He proclaimed, "REPENT".

To repent means to change your way of thinking. Repentance is not a 'spiritual' activity in the sense of coming to a church altar to confess your misdeeds... It is a product of consistent, daily mental effort and decision-making which impacts upon and changes your behaviour. And when your behaviour changes... your life changes!

Someone once defined insanity as continuing to do exactly the same things and expecting a different result. If you want different results, you must be willing to try a different approach, which means you must be willing to think about your situation or circumstance with a fresh mental attitude.

Albert Einstein, the eminent scientist, once stated that, "you cannot solve a problem at the same level at which it was created". You must therefore be willing to rise to a higher level of thinking in order to raise the level of your quality of living.

In an account of Christ's healing of a paralytic man, we see an example of Jesus, the Christ, always seeking to address the deficient thinking He encountered within many of His listeners.

"*...Immediately Jesus knew in his spirit that this was what they were thinking in their hearts, and he said to them, "Why are you thinking these things?"*"[72]

In essence, Jesus was stating that their thinking pattern was a barrier to their understanding and experiencing the fullness of life available to every human. After He rebuked their faulty thinking, He proceeded to demonstrate the power of His Kingdom.

Spend more time with the greatest source of truth, the Bible. Study it with the help of the Holy Spirit, not as a book of religious dogma but as a manual for effective living, seeking within its pages for "*whatever is true, whatever is noble, whatever is right, whatever is pure, whatever is lovely, and whatever is admirable, if anything is excellent or praiseworthy...*"[73]

As you think about such things that you glean from the scriptures, you will find it providing principles and precepts that will equip you to rise to a new level of matured, successful Kingdom living.

PRAY WITHOUT CEASING

In Luke 18: 1 – 8, Jesus "*told his disciples a parable to show them that they should always pray and not give up*". His admonition is just as relevant to us today as we each seek to fulfil God's divine purpose for our lives.

In addition to understanding the message of that parable, it is important to be reminded of the following words of our King and Lord:

"*When a strong man, fully armed, guards his own palace, his goods are in peace. But when a stronger than he comes upon him and overcomes him, he takes from him all his armour in which he trusted, and divides his spoils.*"[74]

In essence, in order for you to release your greatness, you must prepare for a fight. Satan will not willingly give up all he has stolen from you, so you must be prepared to enforce the executive order from the heavenly courts to pursue, overtake and recover all the blessings that already belong to you in the spiritual realm.

And that means a commitment to pray without ceasing.

In the parable referred to above, Jesus shows us three principles that underlay effective, life-transforming, destiny-fulfilling prayer:

Clarity of Purpose – The woman in the parable had a clear understanding of what she wanted to accomplish. She wanted justice (her citizenship rights) and would not be distracted from fulfilling that objective. Similarly, you need to clearly identify and clarify those of your rights as a citizen of God's kingdom that must be fulfilled this year. This means discovering, refining and documenting your vision and goals for the year.

Boldness – She was bold enough to demand her rights from the judge. In much the same way, we can have the boldness and, "*confidence to enter the Most Holy Place by the blood of Jesus, by a new and living way opened for* *us through the curtain, that is, his body, and since we have a great priest over the house of God, let us draw near to God with a sincere heart in full assurance of faith, having our hearts sprinkled to cleanse us from a guilty conscience and having our bodies washed with pure water."*[75]

Persistence – The woman simply would not give up. That is the indomitable spirit of a champion that you must cultivate in order to recover all that God has for you.

As you engage in productive, destiny-oriented efforts and pray without ceasing, you can be assured that He who promised is faithful to bring you into the fullness of His purpose for your life today and in the days to come.

THE VALUE OF TIME

Solomon, the wise king once proclaimed, "*To every thing there is a season, and a time to every purpose under the heaven.*"[76]

Just as the pound is the currency of Great Britain and the dollar is the currency of the United States of America, time may be described as the currency of life.

Time is the primary gift that God has given to every human. Each of us then takes that time and exchanges it for everything else that we currently have in our lives.

For example, if you hold a university degree, you have exchanged about 3 or 4 years of your life for that certificate hanging on your wall.

If you work in a job, you are exchanging each hour of your life for the wage or salary that your employer is willing to pay you for the time spent as her employee.

If you have an excellent relationship with your friend or family member, it is a reflection of the investment of your time in cultivating their friendship.

Everything you are or that you have is measurable in portions of time, which you have dedicated, either directly or indirectly, towards acquiring it. Conversely, anything you do not yet have, it is because you have been unwilling to exchange the relevant amount of time necessary to acquire it.

The celebration of Christ's resurrection during Easter is a tremendous time for every human to reflect on the great work of love Christ did, in order to restore us to citizenship in His kingdom. Understanding and applying the message of the resurrection releases tremendous power into our lives to go forth, slay all opposing mental and spiritual giants, and recover all that God has purposed for our lives.

However, life transformation is a process, not an event. Are you willing to pay the price in effort, the pursuit of wisdom and continued time investment necessary to take you to the next level of success?

Remember the words of the apostle, "*Look carefully then how you walk! Live purposefully and worthily and accurately, not as the unwise and witless, but as wise (sensible, intelligent people), making the very most of the time [buying up each opportunity], because the days are evil. Therefore, do not be vague and thoughtless and foolish, but understanding and firmly grasping what the will of the Lord is.*"[77]

How you spend your time over the next few months will determine whether you maximise the benefits obtained from the resurrection message. Make each moment count towards the fulfilment of the divine purpose for which God has called you into being.

TRUTH THAT SETS FREE

In one of the most well-known passages in the Bible, Jesus the Christ provided the solution to every single problem you are currently experiencing or may ever experience.

Unfortunately, the solution eludes a body of people who, by all accounts, should be the greatest expression of abundant life on the planet. Jesus declared that He had come to give 'life and life more abundantly' to all who follow him and yet, if truth be told, many Christians are held bound in financial, emotional, physical and even spiritual 'straitjackets'.

And the reason is simple...we ignore the solution that the King has provided. Jesus said, *"If you hold to my teaching, you are really my disciples. Then you will know the truth, and the truth will set you free"*[78]

It is important to understand that there are specific principles in God's Kingdom for generating financial success, maintaining emotional stability, strengthening your relationships, enhancing physical health and attaining spiritual maturity.

Many Christians attempt to substitute praying, singing, clapping, church activities and other myriad so-called 'spiritual' endeavours for the acquisition of these principles and its consistent application to their lives but this is merely an exercise in futility.

You see, if God rewards your violation of His kingdom principles, then that would violate His integrity and make Him unholy. Therefore, He cannot reward your financial ignorance with financial blessing, nor can He reward your abuse of health principles with physical well-being... Because He is forever holy!

Freedom from impoverishment in any area of our lives must therefore come from knowledge of the truth as it relates to that dimension of life.

God wants us to experience total peace, joy and success here on earth but He will not force knowledge into our heads. He invites us to partake of wisdom that will bring us into complete liberty but the response of many Christians is captured in these words:

"Wisdom calls aloud in the street, she raises her voice in the public squares; at the head of the noisy streets she cries out, in the gateways of the city she makes her speech. 'How long will you simple ones love your simple ways? How long will mockers delight in mockery and fools hate knowledge? If you had responded to my rebuke, I would have poured out my heart to you and made my thoughts known to you.'" [79]

Today, if you will hear His voice, take a close look at any area of your life, where there is lack and commit to the pursuit and application of godly knowledge in that area. Only then will you experience the freedom that our King has promised you.

THE SPIRIT OF DILIGENCE

Almost three thousand years ago, King Solomon, endowed with supernatural wisdom from God Almighty, expressed a key principle for achieving success in the following words:

"Do you see a man diligent in his business? He shall stand before kings; he shall not stand before ordinary men."[80]

"He becomes poor who works with a slack and idle hand, but the hand of the diligent makes rich."[81]

The attitude or spirit of diligence is one of the key attributes that is common to every truly successful individual or group of people and distinguishes the tremendously successful people from mediocre ones.

Diligence is defined as 'constant in effort to accomplish something or attentive and persistent in doing something'. This implies that diligence is an attitude, characterised by persistence, focus and attention to detail.

Unfortunately, too many people have not cultivated the spirit of diligence and have become victims of poverty in their relationships, in their finances, in their health and other areas of life. Simply put, despite all the Scriptures they quote or positive affirmations they make, many give up too easily when the going gets tough.

They give up on the exercise regime and nutritional discipline required to maintain good health. They discard relationships because someone offends them. They give up on educational studies because they failed one course and on and on the story goes.

Dale Carnegie, one of the most influential writers of the 20th century, once stated the truth that "most of the important things in the world have been accomplished by people who have kept on trying when there seemed to be no hope at all".

Dear friend, if you desire to accomplish all that God desires for you this year, you must cultivate and strengthen the spirit of diligence. Even in the arena of spiritual growth, God reveals that, "*Without faith it is impossible to please him: for he that comes to God must believe that He is, and that He is a rewarder of them that **diligently seek** him.*"[82]

Notice that God does not reward the casual seeker but the diligent one. Similarly, as you pay close attention to the secrets of effective living that God is revealing to you, remain focussed and persistent in the pursuit of His purpose for your life and you will ultimately enjoy the rewards of diligence – Divine Success!

HE HEARS YOUR CRIES

At some point in every human existence and in your walk with The LORD, you will feel like the psalmist felt when he penned the following words:

"My God, my God, why have you forsaken me? Why are you so far from saving me, so far from the words of my groaning? O my God, I cry out by day, but you do not answer, by night, and am not silent…"[83]

Perhaps you are presently at that point….

If so, be assured that God, who loves you with an everlasting love, wants you to understand that the reason you are reading this right now is because, He heard your cries and He is attentive to the wailings of your heart.

He has promised that, even though you may sometimes feel lonely, you are never alone. Beside you, walks the ever-present Holy Spirit who comforts us in all our tribulations.

In addition, whether you know it or not, someone, somewhere is praying for you.

At least three people interceded for you today to help bring you through the dark season you may be experiencing.

- When you whispered in your heart about your situation, God set in motion the answers to your questions because *"He who searches our hearts knows the mind of the Spirit, because the Spirit intercedes for the saints in accordance with God's will."*[84]

- Jesus, The Christ, who sits at the right hand of our heavenly Father, got involved and wants you to know that He is determined *"to save completely those who come to God through him, because he always lives to intercede for them.*"[85]

- And, as these words were written, a prayer went up for you that you would experience the reality of the psalmist's words: "*The LORD is near unto all them that call upon him, to all that call upon him in truth. He will fulfil the desire of them that fear him: he also will hear their cry, and will save them.*"[86]

Dear friend, God is on your side and He will bring you into victory... Simply keep on walking through... the valley of the shadows of despair... and you will emerge into the bright sunshine of God's loving favour and renewed joy because He heard you when you called.

THE JOURNEY

A wise man once said, "Whatever you tolerate, you cannot change". This idea is relevant whether it relates to the behaviour of your children, the problems in your local community, the inadequate performance or attitude of your work colleague or indeed your own personal habits impeding your success.

Until you become dissatisfied enough with the status quo to want to make a change… nothing changes.

Understanding the great responsibility this places upon you demands that you periodically ask yourself this question, "Where are you?"

It is a crucial question that God asked mankind in their first encounter after Adam had disobeyed God's instructions (see Genesis 3: 9).

Imagine that you are on your way to a friend's home for a social engagement and someone phones to ask the question, "Where are you?" This question implies that:

a) There is a desired or correct location or destination where you ought to be.

b) You are not at that destination.

c) Someone is expecting you at that destination.

d) That person believes that you can get there.

e) Someone knows the way to your destination and can direct you.

f) You must be willing to accept the directions.

g) You have to make some changes in order to reach your destination.

These are fundamental steps that also apply to your journey towards the divine purpose for which God called you into planet earth.

God has a destination for you... your purpose for being. He has put milestones in place to enable you check how you are making progress towards your destiny and when you are delayed, or take a wrong turning and don't arrive at the expected location at the appropriate time, He will ring a call through to your spirit and ask, "Where are you?"

How you answer that question will then determine the next phase of your journey and whether you will indeed arrive at your destination. Any insincere or incorrect answers will only lead to self-delusion and further delays.

In the arena of your spiritual growth, Paul the Apostle admonishes, "*Examine yourselves to see whether you are in the faith; test yourselves. Do you not realise that Christ Jesus is in you — unless, of course, you fail the test?*"[87]

This principle of honest self-examination applies to every area of successful human endeavour.

Praise... Your Gateway into Victory

The wise king of Israel once wrote, *"Sing joyfully to the LORD, you righteous; it is fitting for the upright to praise him."*[88]

One of the most rewarding components of the life of an effective citizen of God's Kingdom is the understanding and consistent expression of a lifestyle of praise.

As a child of God, it is important to recognise that praise is not simply something you do in church on a Sunday morning; it is an intrinsic manifestation of who we are on the inside.

You have heard it said that every tree bears fruit according to its kind. That idea is also true of your life as a believer in Christ. When your innermost being is filled with the love, joy and presence of the Holy Spirit, the natural fruit of this is love towards your fellow human and constant praise to the Source and Sustainer of your joy.

Conversely, if the fruit of genuine love and heartfelt praise is missing from your life, then you have to critically examine what tree has taken root in your soul.

There are some tremendous benefits, which follow closely in the footsteps of praise such as:

a) It lifts your spirit above the clouds of despair when you are faced with challenges. Praise corrects your focus from the problem to the Ultimate Source of Solutions.

   It is said that a person's life moves in the direction of your most dominant thoughts. If your thoughts are continually fixed on the problem, your life remains mired in defeat. However, when you enter a fresh dimension of praise, this centres your mind on God and His ability to bring you through.

b) This refocusing unleashes your creativity as it enables you to think 'outside the box' of crisis. The psalmist proclaims, "*I will praise the LORD, who counsels me; even at night my heart instructs me.*"[89] Understandably, when God counsels you, He gives you uncommon wisdom to overcome any challenge.

c) Praise invites the intervention of God and places the resources of His Kingdom at your disposal. The psalmist again puts it this way, "*From the lips of children and infants you have ordained praise [or strength] because of your enemies, to silence the foe and the avenger.*"[90]

Friend, let your praise ring out today and always; it is the gateway into God's presence, and from there into your victory.

SOMETHING UNIQUE IN YOUR LIFE...

Something in your life holds the key to your success...

That may sound like a bold statement but it captures the essence of the principle of 'potential' and fulfilment in the kingdom of God.

The challenge is that many people are either ignorant of the golden deposit within them or massively undervalue it. As a result, they seek here and there, going from one church service to the next, hoping that someone will give them that which they seek.

However, listen to the words of the ultimate leader, Jesus the Christ:

'Once, having been asked by the Pharisees when the kingdom of God would come, Jesus replied, "The kingdom of God does not come with signs to be observed or with visible display", nor will people say, 'Here it is,' or 'There it is,' because the kingdom of God is within you."'[91]

God placed the secret of success where it is impossible for the discerning to miss it... within you.

Every human came to this planet, loaded with unique gifting, characteristics and abilities, which God placed within you in order for you to fulfil His specific assignment. Joseph had his ability to interpret dreams, Daniel had his capacity to organise and administrate, Paul had the power to communicate verbally and in writing, Moses had his Shepherd's rod and leadership ability, David had his musical gift to compose songs and play instruments.

Each one of them was unique and deployed their unique potential for the benefit of their community and brought glory and honour to God, the source of their gifting. Similarly dear friend, something in your life awaits your discovery and deployment for the benefit of this generation.

Have you taken the time to explore who you really are? Have you considered the answers to these five great questions of human existence?

Who am I?	– Your Identity
Where did I come from and what does this mean?	– Your Heritage
What can I do?	– Your Potential
Why am I here?	– Your Purpose
Where am I going?	– Your Destiny

Until you possess clear answers to these questions, life is a careless experiment, flitting around and winding down without accomplishing God's assignment for your existence.

My earnest prayer is that you will seek God's answers to these critical questions and then live your life, henceforth, in such a way that, like our King, you may end your race on earth with those profound words "*It is finished*!"

A HEART FOR GOD

The Apostle Paul was a man whose life characterised selfless service for the cause of the Kingdom of God. Some of his life experiences read like a litany of suffering, ranging from shipwrecks to snakebites, from severe beatings to betrayal by others, from physical affliction to imprisonment.

Perhaps his experiences remind you of some of the challenges you have faced or may be facing. If so, be encouraged... because Paul's experiences did not lead him into bitterness against God or against humanity. Instead, they brought him into a deeper awareness of the love of Christ that is shed abroad in our hearts by the Holy Spirit.

The recognition that Christ's love was sufficient to sustain him through the tough times of life is reflected in his proclamation:

"Who shall separate us from the love of Christ? Shall trouble or hardship or persecution or famine or nakedness or danger or sword? "As it is written: "for your sake we face death all day long; we are considered as sheep to be slaughtered. "No, in all these things we are more than conquerors through him who loved us.

For I am convinced that neither death nor life, neither angels nor demons, neither the present nor the future, nor any powers, neither height nor depth, nor anything else in all creation, will be able to separate us from the love of God that is in Christ Jesus our Lord."[92]

Dear friend, whatever life throws at you, one thing must remain settled in your spirit: you must have a heart that is set on God! All trials and tribulations are transient, compared to the eternal love that Christ Jesus has for you, so you must remain focussed on Him.

Cultivate a heart like David, the beloved king of Israel, who sang:

"O God, you are my God, earnestly I seek you; my soul thirsts for you, my body longs for you, in a dry and weary land where there is no water. I have seen you in the sanctuary and beheld your power and your glory. Because your love is better than life, my lips will glorify you. I will praise you as long as I live, and in your name, I will lift up my hands.... My soul clings to you; your right hand upholds me."[93]

Such a heart, enraptured by God's love, will in turn overflow in love towards all whose lives touch yours.

RETURNING TO YOUR FIRST LOVE

Do you remember what it was like when you first received Jesus Christ into your life as Saviour? The joy that filled your heart, the sense of tranquillity in your soul, the feeling of lightness arising from the burden of sin lifted off your shoulders.

Do you remember the sheer delight of being in God's presence? The longing to share His love in your heart with everyone you met... The ardent desire to pray and study the Bible and know more about the One who loves you with an everlasting love and gave His life to redeem you back from the clutches of Satan, the enemy of your soul.

Do you remember? And is this still how you feel?

Or has it faded into a distant memory, overshadowed by the daily routines of living and your fulfilment of your weekly religious quota of church activities?

If so, Listen Up!

"These are the words of him who holds the seven stars in his right hand and walks among the seven golden candlesticks: I know your deeds, your hard work and your perseverance. I know that you cannot tolerate wicked men, that you have tested those who claim to be apostles but are not, and have found them false. You have persevered and have endured hardships for my name, and have not grown weary.

Yet I hold this against you: You have forsaken your first love. Remember the height from which you have fallen! Repent and do the things you did at first. If you do not repent, I will come to you and remove your candlestick from its place. But you have this in your favour: You hate the practices of the Nicolaitans, which I also hate. He, who has an ear, let him hear what the Spirit says to the churches. To him who overcomes, I will give the right to eat from the tree of life, which is in the paradise of God."[94]

God wants you to be an overcomer; He wants you to step aside from the noise of life and draw nearer to Him, to experience a fresh touch of His loving presence and hear the words of truth and wisdom, reserved for those in close intimacy with Him.

Will you hear what the Spirit is saying to you today?

God has so much more for you in His Kingdom but this will come from knowing Him more intimately... This is why the Holy Spirit wants you to return to your first love.

THE HOTLINE

An ambassador is the physical embodiment of one nation in a foreign land. When you meet an ambassador, you are not meeting an individual; you are meeting an entire nation.

The Bible describes citizens of the Kingdom of God in the following words, "*We are therefore Christ's ambassadors, as though God were making his appeal through us.*"[95] Therefore, when I meet you as a believer in Christ, I am meeting, not an individual, but an ambassador who embodies the Kingdom of Heaven on earth.

Sitting on the desk of the official Ambassador of every nation is either a green or a red coloured phone, which is essentially the 'hotline' to the supreme executive authority in the nation, which may be the Prime Minister, the President or the King. For example, the Ambassador of the United Kingdom to Russia speaks only to the Prime Minister on that phone.

When that phone goes, the Ambassador knows it can be only one specific person on the other end of the line.

Your heavenly Father, the King of the Universe, has planted you in your current location in this generation to pursue and accomplish the interests of His Kingdom on the earth. In order to do this effectively, like the Ambassador of the United Kingdom to Russia, you also have a hotline to the supreme executive authority of the Kingdom.

That hotline is located in the secret place of prayer.

In essence, your prayer room is the Ambassador's office where you obtain the King's instructions. The King himself put it this way, "*My sheep hear my voice, and I know them and they follow Me.*"[96]

Every Ambassador's 'hotline' is fitted with encryption devices to ensure that hostile forces do not intercept the conversation between the Ambassador and the Prime Minister.

Similarly, your hotline is fitted with an encryption device. It is described this way, *"For he that speaks in an unknown tongue speaks not unto men, but unto God: for no man understands him; howbeit in the spirit he speaks mysteries."*[97]

If an Ambassador decides that he is not going to use the hotline, his effectiveness will be significantly impaired because:

a) He will not know the mind of the leader.

b) He will probably make utterances or undertake activities that jeopardise the interests of his nation in the foreign land.

And that characterises a believer who ignores the prayer 'hotline'. If you desire to be effective as an Ambassador of the Kingdom, a lifestyle of prayer is non-negotiable.

THE SEED OF THE RIGHTEOUS

Most Christians are aware that the Bible is full of many promises, which we can appropriate in order to enjoy the manifold blessings that our heavenly Father has made available to us as His children and citizens of His Kingdom.

However, one thing that is clear in God's Word, the Bible, is that many of His promises come with conditions that we are required to fulfil in order to partake of those blessings.

Another thing that is also clear from His Word is that God reveals Himself as a generational thinking Father. When He engages with a man, He is always looking beyond the individual to extend His relationship into future generations with his descendants.

This is why, for example, we have come to know Him as the God of Abraham, Isaac and Jacob.

Understanding this principle places a great responsibility on us as believers in Christ who are in covenant with our Heavenly Father. The responsibility is this:

Whatever you do now has benefits or consequences, not just for yourself but also for your descendants. Whatever seeds you are sowing now, be assured that your future generations, born or yet unborn will reap the fruit thereof.

That is a sobering thought that ought to make the decision to walk in holiness and righteousness much easier for you.

God's word promises, *"Though hand join in hand, the wicked shall not be unpunished: but the seed of the righteous shall be delivered."*[98]

A wise king also observed, "*I have been young, and now am old; yet have I not seen the righteous forsaken, nor his seed begging bread.*"[99]

Righteousness means doing the right thing according to God's revealed standards and thereby remaining in right alignment with His authority and government in your life. It is a daily commitment to live by the laws of God.

Therefore, dear friend, always bear in mind, "*Let us not be weary in well doing: for in due season we shall reap, if we faint not. As we have therefore opportunity, let us do good unto all men, especially unto them who are of the household of faith.*"[100]

Your righteousness positions you, your children and theirs to enjoy the tremendous blessings that God desires for them to enjoy. Indeed, it is safe to say that righteousness is the best legacy you can leave for your family because the seed of the righteous shall be blessed.

RISING ABOVE IT ALL

A fundamental principle that wise men in ancient times and in modern days have understood and applied in their achievement of success is the knowledge that a person's life inevitably moves in the direction of his or her most dominant thoughts.

In essence, what you focus on determines your life outcomes.

If you want to attain or retain emotional balance, maintain physical well-being and achieve continued spiritual growth, then focussing your mind on TV soap operas or talk shows, the daily catalogue of bad news reports and other characteristics of a dysfunctional society portrayed in mass media will not be helpful.

If you focus your mind on defeat, mediocrity or lack, no matter how much you pretend to others about your great faith, time will ultimately reveal the fruit of your mind by the results you produce.

If, on the other hand, you continually focus your mind on victory, excellence and abundance in all dimensions of your life... no matter what your current circumstances may be... time will also reveal the fruit of your mind.

This is why the ultimate manual for successful living, the Holy Bible, regularly encourages us about focussing our minds on appropriate things.

The Apostle Paul, in his letter to the Philippians, provided a list of virtuous attributes upon which we can focus our minds if we are serious about spiritually-sound success (see Philippians 4: 18).

Today, if you feel tired of just being average or if you truly desire to step off the wearying treadmill of mundane life pursuits and religious activity that lacks true fulfilment of your God-ordained purpose, then heed the following words of the wise prophet:

"Have you not known? Have you not heard? The everlasting God, the LORD, The Creator of the ends of the earth, neither faints nor is weary. His understanding is unsearchable. He gives power to the weak, and to those who have no might He increases strength.

Even the youths shall faint and be weary, and the young men shall utterly fall, but those who wait on the LORD shall renew their strength; They shall mount up with wings like eagles, they shall run and not be weary, they shall walk and not faint"[101]

God has called you to sit in heavenly places in Christ Jesus; the key to taking your place in this lofty realm is focussing your mind on pursuing God, His Kingdom, His wisdom and His righteousness.

This is the surest way to rising above all the chaos of modern-day society.

Pursuing Righteousness

Sitting on a mountain, addressing thousands of prospective citizens, Christ Jesus, the Ultimate King, outlined some fundamental requirements for living life effectively in His kingdom. One of the essential requirements was captured in these words:

"Blessed are they who hunger and thirst after righteousness; for they shall be filled."[102]

Righteousness may be defined as right positioning with governmental authority through proper personal conduct and disposition.

A careful examination of the words of the Master shown above, however, highlights two key principles, which are important for us as citizens of God's Kingdom.

   a) **Your decisions determine your future** – You determine your positioning with God through your choice to hunger after Him or not.

   b) **Passion and Pursuit triggers a divine response** – Hunger and thirst are not casual human appetites. These are the life sustaining needs that must be satisfied if you are to survive as a human on earth.

What happens to the human body when hunger and thirst are not satisfied? It will eventually shrivel up and die. So evidently, when He commands us to seek as a matter of topmost priority, the Kingdom of God and His righteousness (see Matthew 6: 33), Jesus is not talking about a casual, laid-back, lackadaisical approach to the presence of God or His rule in our lives.

Jesus the Christ, our King, is saying to us that only a heart that actively pursues, craves and desires right positioning with God so much that if it is not satisfied, it will shrivel and die, attracts the response of Heaven.

So, this raises the inevitable question; how much do you really want His righteousness in your life?

The answer is not revealed by your lips but by what you did yesterday and the day before and the day before that and what you will do after you finish reading this, today, tomorrow and the days after.

The answer will be revealed by whether you spend your time engaged in religious activities, entertainment, career success, personal fame and fortune or whatever else catches your fancy, at the expense of pursuing knowledge of His truths in the Scriptures and quality time in His glorious presence. That is the true test of your desire for God's righteousness...

Heaven awaits your answer!

TRUST IN THE LORD

Thousands of years ago, a very wise king gave a simple admonition, which still holds true today for anyone who is intent on attaining and maintaining the God kind of success.

Solomon advised, "*Trust in the LORD with all your heart and lean not on your own understanding; in all your ways acknowledge Him, and He shall direct your paths. Do not be wise in your own eyes; fear the LORD and depart from evil. It will be health to your flesh, and strength to your bones.*"[103]

Events in many nations around the world continually serve to reinforce the need to consider and adhere to this wise counsel. Just as government ministers and scientists (national and international) assure us that they have eradicated public health threats, such as foot and mouth disease, SARS virus, pandemic flu, some other threat shows up elsewhere in the world, invalidating their bold claims.

As soon as economists tell us that the global economy is getting stronger, the financial markets and the economy wobble triggered by some crises in a nation, adverse news about the banking sector or other industrial sector, and negate the assurances given by so-called experts.

It is clear to the discerning that we are living in a time of accelerated change and tremendous complexity and all your life decisions, which affect your present and set the foundation for your future, have to be made within such a turbulent context.

In essence, as you seek to make wise choices for you and your loved ones, it is more sensible to seek the counsel of a person who knows all things and put your trust in the only person who can guarantee His promises to you. An ancient sage identified Him in this way:

"God is not a man, that He should lie, nor a son of man, that He should repent. Has He said, and will He not do? Or has He spoken, and will He not make it good?" [104]

Dear friend, now more than ever is the time to return to the place of daily, personal prayer to seek the heart and mind of Christ, who holds the future of all mankind in His hands.

It is a time to understand that human wisdom, however beneficial, has its limitations and making life decisions based on such limitations, when there is a superior alternative, is unnecessary self-deprivation.

God has wonderful thoughts of blessing towards you and wants you to enjoy the best that His Kingdom has to offer. You must, however, be willing to reach beyond reliance on yourself or your fellow mortal man to place your trust in the Lord.

IT'S NOT OVER

As we enter the latter half or final stretch of any year, many people have generally given up on the dreams and aspirations they had at the beginning of the year.

For some others, the enthusiasm with which they began has waned and they are simply coasting through the rest of the year, living each day with even less passion or sense of purpose than the day before.

Friend, if this happens to you, whenever it does, choose instead to shake off the lethargy that has sapped your emotional, physical and spiritual strength and rekindle your quest to accomplish all that God has earmarked for you.

There is a clarion call ringing out from the throne room of the King and His admonition is this… Do not give up on the dream that God has placed within your heart!

It is indeed your season to achieve superlative success but you must maintain a spirit of resilience. Christ, our King proclaimed, *"No man, having put his hand to the plough, and looking back, is fit for the kingdom of God."*[105]

Dr Robert Schuller once said, "When the going gets tough, the tough get going," which is the attitude that winners cultivate to see them through those seasons when things are not working according to plan.

Above all, as a child of God, you have access to a reservoir of dynamic power that you can tap into, to lift you above the clouds of weariness. That reservoir is found in God who *"…gives power to the faint; and to them that have no might he increases strength. Even the youths shall faint and be weary, and the young men shall utterly fall: But they that wait upon the LORD shall renew their strength; they shall mount up with wings as eagles; they shall run, and not be weary; and they shall walk, and not faint."*[106]

God took Esther from orphan to Queen of Persia in one day, Joseph from prison to Prime Minister of Egypt in one day and Christ Jesus, our ultimate leader, from the despair of the cross to the triumph of eternal dominion in one day.

During the final months of any year, cultivate the practice of raising your expectancy level. Understand that your victory could be right around the corner and could happen very fast.

The same God who brought Esther, Joseph and Christ into great victory *"is able to do immeasurably more than all we ask or imagine, according to his power that is at work within us"*[107] and He wants you to know that it is not over until you win!

RETURNING TO THE FOUNTAIN

There is a place where your soul finds perfect rest, where you are at complete peace and time seems to stand still. It is a place where the burdens roll off your shoulders and the cares and pressures of life are a very distant memory.

It is a place where your whole being is suffused with joy and you experience a sense of complete liberty.

When you are there, nothing else matters, only the one with whom you are there. And that place is?

The presence of the LORD!

No one needs to announce it when you are in His presence... You simply know it! And if anyone says to you, "the presence of The LORD is here", you will also know whether it is true or not because here is what the Bible says about His presence:

"*You will show me the path of life: in your presence is fullness of joy; at your right hand there are pleasures for evermore.*"[108]

"*Suddenly a sound like the blowing of a violent wind came from heaven and filled the whole house where they were sitting. They saw what seemed to be tongues of fire that separated and came to rest on each of them. All of them were filled with the Holy Spirit and began to speak in other tongues as the Spirit enabled them.*"[109]

"*It came even to pass, as the trumpeters and singers were as one, to make one sound to be heard in praising and thanking the LORD; and when they lifted up their voice with the trumpets and cymbals and instruments of music, and praised the LORD, saying, For he is good; for his mercy endures for ever: that then the house was filled with a cloud, even the house of the LORD; So that the priests could not stand to minister by reason of the cloud: for the glory of the LORD had filled the house of God.*"[110]

As you can see, the presence of the LORD makes an extraordinary impact on all who enter in. And that impacting presence is the source of our power to influence and impact our communities and nations as ambassadors of the Kingdom of God.

Friend, resolve to no longer settle for religious self-deception. You must choose to return to the fountain of God's manifest presence, that truly resolves all the questions of your soul, and empowers you for dynamic Kingdom service.

Just as the ancient priests discovered, we enter in through pure, unadulterated worship.

IGNORANCE IS DEADLY

There are some Biblical principles for successful living that many Christians quote, but evidently do not understand. And we know this is so because proof of understanding is evidenced by action, not by mere words. One such principle is found in God's words spoken through the prophet Hosea:

"My people are destroyed from lack of knowledge. Because you have rejected knowledge, I also reject you as my priests. Because you have ignored the law of your God, I also will ignore your children."[111]

From these words, it is clear that ignorance can be very deadly. Ignorance in any area of your life can hurt you and cause you to bring devastation to those around you, including those you love.

Saul was ignorant concerning his assignment on earth and the deity of Jesus Christ. This ignorance kept him from salvation and led him to persecute and bring destruction into the lives of some disciples of Christ. A knowledge encounter reversed that and set him on course to become Paul, the most prolific New Testament writer and ambassador for the Kingdom of God (read Acts 9: 1 – 16).

The formal education system demonstrates clearly that your life transitions from one level to the next according to your knowledge. This also holds true for the universal curriculum of life. This is why we are admonished to, *"Study to show yourself approved unto God, a workman that needs not to be ashamed, rightly handling the word of truth."*[112]

There is, however, a price to pay for the acquisition of knowledge and Godly wisdom. The price is paid in finances, time and effort required to develop your mind. Some people quibble, especially about the financial cost of knowledge but fail to understand that ignorance is infinitely more expensive.

For example, when last did you spend more on good quality book(s) and other educational material than that nice suit or beautiful dress you are wearing?

Your answer will reveal whether you indeed value improving the quality of your mind more than the beauty of your body.

The Bible declares, "*As a man thinks within himself, so is he.*"[113] Therefore, if you are not actively engaged in consistently improving your mind, you are effectively negating the right to expect a better quality of living. Why? Because it is unreasonable to keep going round the same, 'mind roundabout' and expect to arrive at a different destination.

So choose today to avoid the deadly costs of ignorance by the active pursuit of Godly wisdom.

Come Up Higher

The Eagle is called the 'king of birds' because it demonstrates the capacity to live at a higher level than other birds. Whilst chickens and other birds scurry away in fright at the first sign of a strong wind or a storm, the eagle flies into it and rises higher on the currents of those same strong winds.

God has designed every citizen of His Kingdom to be "*the head, and not the tail; and you shall be above only, and you shall not be beneath…*"[114]

He also desires that we manifest our in-built nature as eagles just as He proclaimed through Isaiah, the prophet, that "*But they that wait upon the LORD shall renew their strength; they shall mount up with wings as eagles…*"[115]

In this world, filled with social, economic, religious, political and many other forms of turmoil, there is a clarion call for strong, quality people, able to rise on the strong winds of turbulence to provide leadership to our communities and nations.

Our world needs you to respond to the same call of the Spirit, which He gave to the apostle John, "*Come up higher and I will show you what must take place after this.*"[116]

When you have one of the most senior police officers in the United Kingdom calling for the legalisation of hard drugs like cocaine and heroin, which are proven to be destructive to their users and to society in general, it is evident that the challenges of our generation will not be solved by earthly wisdom.

Every believer, and that includes you… yes you… needs to step out of the shade of religious activities, that merely numb the senses and provide temporary satisfaction, into a fresh reality of God's powerful presence that makes us dangerous adversaries to the kingdom of darkness.

Are you willing to rise as an eagle? Are you willing to soar in the heavenly places with the Holy Spirit? Are you willing to make more of a difference to your community? Then come on up higher, in the place of personal prayer.

God wants each and every one of us to step into a higher dimension of His Spirit where we can clearly hear His voice and see His plans for our nations and our world. Then He wants you to step into society as His agent of change who will declare and fulfil the mandate, "*Your Kingdom come, Your will be done on earth as it is in heaven.*"[117]

It is Time!

THOUGHT MANAGEMENT

Many Christians are familiar with the principle articulated in Proverbs 23: 7 that *"As a man thinks in his heart, so is he."*

Even though many people, including Christians, try to abdicate this responsibility, these words from The LORD, spoken through the wise king Solomon, essentially places the responsibility for your life squarely on your shoulders.

In order to fulfil this responsibility properly and complete the divine assignment for which our Creator placed you on this planet, Solomon's words indicate that you have to manage your thoughts effectively.

Paul, the Apostle, reinforced this idea when he admonished, *"Finally, brethren, whatsoever things are true, whatsoever things are honest, whatsoever things are just, whatsoever things are pure, whatsoever things are lovely, whatsoever things are of good report; if there be any virtue, and if there be any praise, think on these things."*[118]

In essence, both of these exemplary leaders in the Kingdom of God advocate that thought management is a fundamental key to successful living.

What sort of life do you really want?

One, which is marked by mediocrity, failure, spiritual weakness, emotional dysfunction and physical deprivation? Alternatively, one characterised by tremendous success, spiritual well-being, financial blessings and emotional balance?

Well, the challenge is that you never really choose those results… you choose the thought patterns that create the actions, which ultimately lead to those results.

In-depth Bible study sessions provide an excellent opportunity for you to explore the wisdom of God. The prime benefit of pursuing and learning the wisdom of God from His Word is that it changes and realigns your thinking with the ageless truths that create a life of eternal success.

The Apostle Paul again encourages us, *"Do not conform any longer to the pattern of this world, but be transformed by the renewing of your mind. Then you will be able to test and approve what God's will is—his good, pleasing and perfect will."*[119]

As you step into this week, ask yourself each day, "What area of my life needs to be transformed? This should in turn lead to the foundational question, "What area of my thinking needs to be renewed?

Answering these questions honestly will position you to step into a new realm of thinking that unleashes the greatest and best that God has for you because the truth of the matter is that thought management is life management.

REACH BEYOND YOUR PAST

One of the fundamental benefits of obtaining citizenship in a new country is the opportunity to literally begin again. Ask anyone who has endured the challenges of being an immigrant in the United Kingdom or other nation and finally secures the right to stay permanently. They will definitely attest to the fact that the day they secured their permanent residence or citizenship of their new nation was indeed a day of great rejoicing, one in which they secured a new lease on life with rights and privileges previously unavailable to them.

Every person who chooses to submit to the lordship of Christ also enjoys this tremendous benefit because your decision for Christ does not turn you into a member of a religious club called Christianity; it literally translates you into a new country... the Kingdom of God, and *"if any man be in Christ, he is a new creature: old things are passed away; behold all things are become new."*[120]

One of the privileges of this is that God does not consult your past to determine your future. He buries your past where it belongs... in the past!

And so should you...

Consider a prostitute named Rahab. Based on her past, most people would not naturally consider her as a suitable candidate for being an ancestor to three of the greatest people in human history.

Yet God looked beyond her past into her future and reserved a place for her where history can never ignore her... as a maternal ancestor of King David, King Solomon and Jesus the Christ, the King of all kings.

God has a future, so big, in store for you that its brilliance would dazzle even you, if only you would dare to remove the sunshade of past failures and weaknesses, through which you choose to view what is possible in your future.

God Himself admonishes, "*Do not remember the former things, nor consider the things of old. Behold, I will do a new thing, now it shall spring forth; shall you not know it? I will even make a road in the wilderness and rivers in the desert.*"[121]

Where your past was marked by the wilderness of confusion, personal failure and spiritual dryness, God is leading you onto a highway of victory and spiritual refreshing.

But He will not force you to take the journey... you must be willing to reach beyond your past, take each step with Him daily and emerge into a new dimension of godly, effective living.

The Proof of Love

The central commandments that God has given us to live by are captured in the following encounter that Jesus Christ, our King, had with one of the leaders of ancient Israel:

"And one of the scribes came, and having heard them reasoning together, and perceiving that he had answered them well, asked him, which is the first commandment of all?

And Jesus answered him, the first of all the commandments is, Hear, O Israel; The Lord our God is one Lord: And you shall love the Lord your God with all your heart, and with all your soul, and with all your mind, and with all your strength: this is the first commandment. And the second is like it, namely this; you shall love your neighbour as yourself. There is no other commandment greater than these."[122]

Having understood that love for God and love for your neighbour is God's primary expectation of anyone who is serious about their citizenship in the Kingdom of God, how then do you know that you are fulfilling this requirement?

Is it by spending time in church or trying to impress others with songs, prayers and assertions that, "Jesus is Lord" to anyone willing to listen?

Well, the King says, *"Not everyone who says to me, 'Lord, Lord,' will enter the kingdom of heaven..."*[123]

So how do you prove your love to the King?

The King Himself gives the answer in the rest of his statement; *"Not everyone who says to me, 'Lord, Lord,' will enter the kingdom of heaven, but only he who does the will of my Father who is in heaven."*[124]

The word translated as 'will' in this passage means original intent, predetermined goal, fundamental objective or predestined purpose.

In essence, according to Jesus, the Christ, our Ultimate Leader, the fulfilment of your God-ordained purpose is the proof of love.

When you discover your purpose and begin to pursue its fulfilment, according to God's pattern, it will inevitably bring benefit to your fellow human beings and you would be fulfilling the second primary requirement of 'loving your neighbour.'

So, the key questions that determine your eternal future are:

- Have you discovered your purpose or assignment on earth?
- Are you pursuing and fulfilling that purpose effectively?

Friend, until you can answer these questions positively, with an absolute sense of conviction, there is no greater objective to which you should be dedicating your time and effort, for therein lies the proof of your love for the King.

YOUR GATEWAY TO POWER

Power is the one thing that every human on the face of the earth craves. However, if you ask them the direct question, "Do you want power?" many religious people, in a show of false humility, will pretend that they don't seek power.

Yet, the only person, who knows the secret desires of every human heart, showed clearly that you don't just want power... you need power.

Listen to the instructions of the Ultimate Leader to those who had walked closest with him during three years of earth transforming ministry:

"And, being assembled together with them, he **commanded them** *that they should not depart from Jerusalem, but wait for the promise of the Father, which, said he, you have heard me speak about.*

For John baptized with water, but in a few days you will be baptized with the Holy Spirit.... **you shall receive power**, *after that the Holy Spirit is come upon you: and you shall be witnesses unto me both in Jerusalem, and in all Judaea, and in Samaria, and unto the uttermost part of the earth."*[125]

Notice that Christ did not suggest to His disciples that they might, perhaps, want to consider remaining in Jerusalem. He commanded them to remain... until they received power.

This implies that Jesus did not consider power to be an optional extra but an integral key to effective, successful living and a critical factor required for us to achieve God's divine purposes as witnesses to the King and the Kingdom of God.

You need power over your circumstances. You yearn for power over financial insufficiency, health problems, emotional turmoil, relationship difficulties and spiritual weakness. You desire to be an overcomer in all areas of your life.

And Christ our King knows that you do... so He sent us the Holy Spirit.

The Holy Spirit is the Source and Sustainer of all the power you need to live effectively on this planet, and beyond, and the measure of power in your life is a direct reflection of the quality of your relationship with Him.

Dear friend, resolve today to begin a closer relationship with the Holy Spirit, which is initiated by first receiving Jesus the Christ into your life as Saviour and Lord,

However, if you are already a Kingdom citizen, invest the time to cultivate (by spending time with God in the secret place of prayer) a stronger relationship with the Holy Spirit, for He is our gateway to power.

THE POWER OF CONVERSATIONS

Success or failure in life begins with a conversation. Every setback can be traced back to a conversation you had, either within yourself or with someone else who convinced you of that action or direction you eventually chose to pursue.

The following event, recorded at the dawn of time, first demonstrated this principle:

'Now the serpent was more crafty than any of the wild animals the LORD God had made. He said to the woman, "Did God really say, 'You must not eat from any tree in the garden'?" The woman said to the serpent, "We may eat fruit from the trees in the garden, but God did say, 'You must not eat fruit from the tree that is in the middle of the garden, and you must not touch it, or you will die.'"

"You will not surely die," the serpent said to the woman. "For God knows that when you eat of it your eyes will be opened, and you will be like God, knowing good and evil." When the woman saw that the fruit of the tree was good for food and pleasing to the eye, and also desirable for gaining wisdom, she took some and ate it. She also gave some to her husband, who was with her, and he ate it."[126]

That was the beginning of mankind's failures and the principle still holds true until today.

To whom are you listening? Whom are you allowing to speak into your heart? Are you constantly engaged in positive, life-enriching, kingdom-expanding, and godly goal-achieving conversations?

Or are your conversations filled with self-limiting talk, doubt, fear, anger, envy, bitterness, gossip about others or other life-diminishing dialogues?

It is important to understand that there is no neutral conversation in life. What you are saying to yourself, to others, or allowing to be said to you is either moving you forward towards the achievement of God's greatest and best for your life, or they are moving you away from their fulfilment.

Our Heavenly Father is always keen to engage in conversations that introduce you to the greatness He has deposited within you. He spoke to Gideon, Moses, Jeremiah, Abraham, Paul, Solomon and many others in the Bible and His conversations moved them to a higher dimension of effectiveness in their lives. Gideon and Moses delivered their people, Abraham founded a nation, Solomon led his kingdom and Paul has impacted many generations.

What could you achieve if you engaged in the right conversations? Try it for the next thirty days and watch your life flourish greatly...

IN HIS TIME

One of the fundamental truths the ancient priests understood about our Heavenly Father is that He is immortal. This is revealed in the following admonition to the saints to... "*Stand up and praise the LORD your God, who is from everlasting to everlasting. Blessed be your glorious name, and may it be exalted above all blessing and praise.*"[127]

Yet, because of His purposes for mankind on earth, He created time by which we may measure and evaluate the effectiveness of our earthly sojourn.

Solomon revealed a simple, yet powerful truth which when fully understood, can translate you into the most dynamic, powerful, productive phase of your life yet.

He said, "*There is a time for everything, and a season for every activity under heaven: a time to be born and a time to die, a time to plant and a time to uproot, a time to kill and a time to heal, a time to tear down and a time to build, a time to weep and a time to laugh.*

A time to mourn and a time to dance, a time to scatter stones and a time to gather them, a time to embrace and a time to refrain... a time to be silent and a time to speak, a time to love and a time to hate, a time for war and a time for peace..."[128]

Solomon's words show clearly that not all things are appropriate at all times, hence the need to understand and cultivate two crucial personal skills:

- **Discernment:** Knowing the right activity for the right season (or time) of your life. This rests upon knowing God's purposes and assignment for you. Or put another way, "if you don't know what you ought to be doing, how will you know when you ought to be doing it?"

- **Preparation:** One key definition of success is, 'the place where opportunity meets preparedness.' One of the greatest tragedies in life is to arrive at your destination unprepared, because your lack of preparation leaves you ill-equipped to walk through the doors of opportunity God has opened for you.

    Friend, choose to cultivate, through intimacy with the Holy Spirit, and through personal consistent effort, those two success skills and the power of this statement, "*He has made every thing beautiful in his time,*"[129] will be more than words to you. They will be your exciting, joyful reality.

LIVING ABOVE SIN

"*For I know the thoughts that I think toward you, says The LORD, thoughts of peace, and not of evil, to give you an expected end.*"[130]

This prophetic declaration, through Jeremiah, captures the very heartbeat of God and His love towards you as a citizen of His Kingdom. God is so committed to accomplishing His promises of blessing, goodness and favour in your life that He will move heaven and earth to ensure their fulfilment. Indeed, God will turn every attempt of evil people to curse you into blessings in your life.

God demonstrated such a commitment when the Moabite enemies of His people Israel tried to destroy them through the power of a curse (read Numbers 22 – 25).

Three times Balaam tried to curse Israel on behalf of Balak, the king of Moab and three times, he failed... "*Then Balak's anger burned against Balaam. He struck his hands together and said to him, 'I summoned you to curse my enemies, but you have blessed them these three times.*"[131]

This episode reveals that your enemies are powerless against you when you are walking in proper alignment with the Kingdom of God and fulfilling your responsibilities as a citizen in good standing.

What happens when you choose a different alternative?

"*While Israel was staying in Shittim, the men began to indulge in sexual immorality with Moabite women, who invited them to the sacrifices to their gods. The people ate and bowed down before these gods. So Israel joined in worshiping the Baal of Peor. And the LORD's anger burned against them.... Those who died in the plague numbered 24,000*"[132]

Evidently, choosing the wrong alternative resulted in destruction.

Just like the Israelites experienced, whatever Satan, the arch-enemy of your soul cannot accomplish through physical, emotional, financial or spiritual attacks, you help him to achieve by choosing to walk in sin.

Walking in holiness or righteousness is therefore not about some religious dogma trying to force you to please God... it is about enlightened self-interest. It is about guaranteeing and protecting your rights to liberty, blessings and prosperity as a Kingdom citizen.

Living above sin is your insurance policy against defeat, at the hands of all spiritual or physical adversaries, because, *"The angel of the LORD encamps round about them that fear Him, and delivers them."*[133]

Choose to make holiness your daily watchword as you pursue all that God has for you in the rest of this year and thereby experience unending victory.

LIFE ETERNAL

One crucial factor that affects decision-making is the timeframe in focus. For example, when politicians are about to contest elections, they make decisions they hope will be popular with the electorate and thereby help them to win the election. However, when there is no election on the horizon, they are apt to make a different set of decisions.

Similarly, people in the business, religious or even the family arena make different sets of decisions based on their timeframe focus. For instance, as Christmas approaches, if you are focussed on the short term, you are likely to make a different set of spending decisions (like maxing out the credit cards) compared to those who might be more focussed on the long term.

Knowing that the quality of your decisions is affected by the timeframe you are focussed on raises this important question:

Are you more focussed on this transient life on earth or are you focussed on eternal life in the Kingdom of God?

Jesus Christ, our ultimate Leader and King, admonishes us to keep our focus in the right place and within the right timeframe through the following words:

"Do not store up for yourselves treasures upon earth, where moth and rust disfigure, and where thieves break in and steal but store up for yourselves treasures in heaven, where neither moth nor rust disfigure, and where thieves do not break in or steal for where your treasure is, there will your heart be also."[134]

Notice that Christ is really addressing the issue of the human heart by making the point that your spending pattern is an excellent measure of where you are located in relation to the Kingdom of God.

His desire for every citizen of His Kingdom to be focussed on eternity is reinforced by the following:

"*My sheep hear my voice, and I know them, and they follow me:* **And I give unto them eternal life;** *and they shall never perish, neither shall any man pluck them out of my hand.*"[135]

"*The one who sows to please his sinful nature, from that nature [or his flesh, from the flesh] will reap destruction; the one who sows to please the Spirit,* **from the Spirit will reap eternal life**."[136]

Dear friend, as you approach each week, ensure that you make room in your heart for the most important decision of each day; the focus on eternal life.

A LITTLE LEAVEN

At regular intervals, it is beneficial to set apart the time to take stock of where you are, in relation to the fulfilment of your divine purpose, and the accomplishment of the goals and dreams that God has placed on your heart.

For many people, this time of reflection may lead you to relate all too closely with the following words from Paul the apostle, "*You were running a good race. Who cut in on you and kept you from obeying the truth?*"[137]

In essence, 'how did it all go so wrong?' Your pursuit of your dreams started with great promise, you were all charged up, ready to face life, ready to achieve tremendous success and do great things for the kingdom of God, but somehow, it all seemed to fizzle out.

Well… Paul provides the answer, by the inspiration of the Holy Spirit as he proclaimed, "*that kind of persuasion does not come from the one who calls you; A little leaven leavens the whole lump.*"[138]

Essentially, Paul highlighted a simple yet profound truth, which is that, somewhere along the way, you absorbed some wrong information that effectively worked its way throughout your belief system and stopped you in your tracks.

You allowed a little leaven (also called yeast) of fear, doubt or sin to creep in and contaminate your walk with The LORD, which in turn rendered the whole loaf of your life to become less effective for God's Kingdom purposes.

Well friend, all is not lost. Today, if you will hear God's voice, "*purge out the old leaven, that you may be a new lump, since you truly are unleavened.*"[139]

Today is a fresh opportunity to REPENT, which means 'to change your thinking'. Discard those thoughts (and resulting behaviours) that have kept you from fulfilling your goals and destiny thus far. Discard the ungodly counsel that suggests it is okay to flirt with sin or the voices that say that you cannot be great for God.

Return to filling your mind with God's unfailing truth and heed the godly counsel that says, *"Do not be conformed to this world, but be transformed by the renewing of your mind that you may prove (experience) what is that good and acceptable and perfect will of God."*[140]

The clarion call has gone out… It is Success Time. So, as you purge out the old leaven, may you enter your coming period, renewed, invigorated, ready and able to maximize your potential and release the greatness within you.

A New You

Welcome to your new season (a new week, new month or new year).

Whatever your last season was like, good or not so good, you now have a new opportunity to look forward and reach higher for greater things in God. Remember that what is excellent at one level is mediocre at the next or as the Bible puts it, "*The path of the righteous is like the shining light that **shines ever brighter** unto the perfect day.*"[141]

Resolve to go for all that God has in store for you, according to His divine plan and purpose for your life, and do not settle for anything less.

However, it is crucial to recognise that stepping into greater dimensions of effective living in your new season demands a new set of choices, because not everything or everyone in your past qualifies for your future.

You must be willing to make the tough choices that will enable you to break free of the limitations of your past and cross the threshold into divinely-ordained fulfilment.

You may need to renew or realign your inner circle of friendships because the old circle has kept your life and the fulfilment of your assignment in stagnation for too long.

Your quest for a better life will demand that you cultivate new success habits, new relationships, new thinking patterns, new skills, new wisdom and indeed a new, vibrant experience with God. Therefore, the question that requires careful consideration is this:

Are you willing to embrace the new?

This is not a reference to the reluctant acceptance of new circumstances forced upon you by life, but a commitment to the dynamic, godly pursuit of freshness in your walk with Christ and in the pursuit of His agenda for your life.

Many people desire a season of new beginnings but will not experience the newness because they choose to ignore Christ's words, "*No one tears a patch from a new garment and sews it on an old one. If he does, he will have torn the new garment, and the patch from the new will not match the old. And no one pours new wine into old wineskins. If he does, the new wine will burst the skins, the wine will run out and the wineskins will be ruined. No, new wine must be poured into new wineskins.*"[142]

In essence, according to the Ultimate Leader, you have a truly new season when you understand that it all begins with a commitment to becoming a new you.

Let the journey begin!

RELEASE YOUR GREATNESS

OTHER BOOKS BY YEMI AKINSIWAJU

THE LEADERSHIP JIGSAW

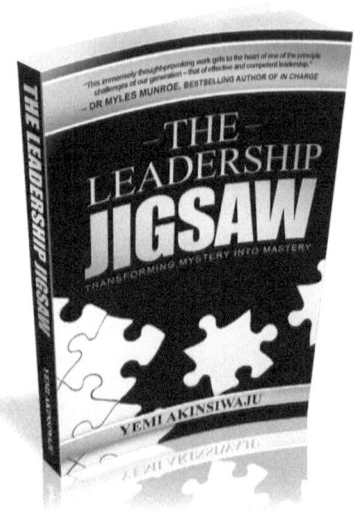

"This immensely thought-provoking work gets to the heart of one of the principle challenges of our generation – that of effective and competent leadership."

~ Dr Myles Munroe

(International Leadership Statesman and Consultant to Governments)

ISBN: 978-0-9934482-1-8   Hardcover
ISBN: 978-0-9934482-0-1   Paperback

Available from Amazon, Barnes and Noble and other good bookstores

SCORECARD

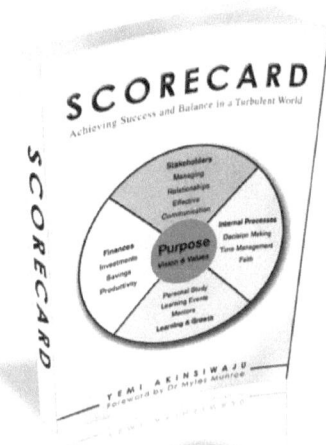

"This has to be one of the best and inspiring books that I have read in the last 2-3 years. I have a new spark for life and a greater zeal to succeed in all that I do. I will give the book to people I meet who express a genuine desire to move from being good to great and are willing to be stretched in all areas of their lives to achieve their goals."

~ Michael Smith MBE

(Award-winning Metropolitan Police Officer and Founder of Word for Weapons, UK)

ISBN:	978-0-59571-354-7	Hardcover
ISBN:	978-0-59547-807-1	Paperback

Available from Amazon.com, Barnes and Noble and other good bookstores

THRIVE! – VOLUME 1

"The insights contained in this book are revelatory, informative, directional and life transforming. Everyone should aspire to read through at least once a year; and refer to it as often as possible."

~ Michael Olawore

(Former Senior Pastor, New Wine Church, London and Global)

ISBN: 978-0-9934482-3-2   Paperback
ISBN: 978-0-9934482-4-9   Hardcover

**Available from Amazon.com, Barnes and Noble
and other good bookstores**

ABOUT THE AUTHOR

YEMI AKINSIWAJU, known as the Leadership Catalyst, is dedicated to enhancing the leadership capacity of individuals and organizations.

Yemi sits on the Board of Directors of the International Third World Leaders Association (ITWLA), an organisation devoted to training and developing leaders in over forty nations. He is the author of the following highly acclaimed books:

- *The Leadership Jigsaw: Transforming Mystery to Mastery*
- *Scorecard: Achieving Success and Balance in a Turbulent World*
- *Thrive: Keys to Enjoying a Life of Purpose and Fulfilment – Vol 1*

Yemi is a multi-gifted international speaker, consultant and author, focussed on the crucial issues of leadership, personal transformation, organisational effectiveness, social and spiritual development. He has addressed audiences from over 50 nations as a conference speaker, seminar facilitator, mentor, trainer, coach and in television and radio appearances.

To find out more about Yemi or to book him to speak at your event, contact him via the details below:

      Email: Yemi@YemiAkinsiwaju.com

      Website: www.YemiAkinsiwaju.com

REFERENCES

1. Genesis 3:8 – 9
2. Proverbs 3: 26
3. Exodus 19: 5
4. Isaiah 1: 19 – 20
5. John 10: 10
6. Lamentations 1: 18
7. Lamentations 3: 7 – 9
8. James 1: 22 – 25
9. Daniel 6: 3
10. Daniel 6: 4
11. Matthew 5: 16
12. Romans 8: 19
13. Matthew 5: 14
14. Ezekiel 22: 30
15. Romans 8: 28
16. Matthew 5: 43 – 48
17. 1 John 4: 20
18. John 4: 24
19. Psalm 84: 10
20. Psalm 16: 11
21. 2 Corinthians 3: 17
22. Jeremiah 29: 13
23. Acts 16: 25 – 26
24. 2 Chronicles 20: 21 – 22
25. Psalm 92: 12 – 15
26. Jeremiah 29: 11
27. Matthew 16: 24 – 25
28. Esther 4: 14
29. Proverbs 4: 23
30. Isaiah 26: 3
31. 2 Corinthians 4: 17 – 18
32. Isaiah 30: 15
33. John 8: 31 – 32
34. James 1: 22 – 25
35. Proverbs 4: 7 – 11
36. Ecclesiastes 1: 9
37. Hosea 4: 6
38. Psalm 139: 14 – 16
39. Luke 17: 11 – 19
40. Psalm 101: 5
41. Psalm 150: 6
42. Philippians 2: 12
43. Matthew 6: 33
44. Matthew 15: 8 – 9
45. Matthew 22: 37 – 40
46. 1 Corinthians 13: 4 – 8
47. See Matthew 5: 13
48. Isaiah 9: 6 – 7
49. Matthew 2: 1
50. Joshua 1: 2 – 9
51. Philippians 1: 6
52. Hebrews 13: 5 – 6
53. Ephesians 2: 10
54. Genesis 1: 26
55. Hebrews 12: 14
56. 2 Corinthians 7: 1
57. Revelation 15: 4a
58. Romans 6: 19
59. Proverbs 4: 23
60. Luke 6: 45
61. Philippians 3: 20 – 21
62. Acts 22: 25 – 29
63. 2 Corinthians 3: 18
64. 2 Corinthians 5: 14 – 17
65. Proverbs 20: 27
66. See John 1:9
67. Matthew 5: 14 – 16
68. Matthew 11: 12
69. Romans 8: 19 – 21
70. 1 Kings 19: 11 – 13
71. Isaiah 30:15
72. Luke 5: 17 – 26

73	Philippians 4: 8	108	Psalm 16: 11
74	Luke 11: 21 – 22	109	Acts 2: 2 – 4
75	Hebrews 10: 19 – 22	110	2 Chronicles 5: 13 – 14
76	Ecclesiastes 3: 1	111	Hosea 4: 6
77	Ephesians 5: 15 – 17 (AMP)	112	2 Timothy 2: 15
78	John 8: 31 – 32	113	Proverbs 23: 7
79	Proverbs 1: 20 – 23	114	Deuteronomy 28: 13a
80	Proverbs 22: 29	115	Isaiah 40: 31
81	Proverbs 10: 4	116	Revelation 4: 1
82	Hebrews 11: 6	117	Matthew 6: 10
83	Psalm 22: 1 – 2	118	Philippians 4: 8
84	Romans 8: 27	119	Romans 12: 2
85	Hebrews 7: 25	120	2 Corinthians 5: 17
86	Psalm 145: 18 – 19	121	Isaiah 43: 18 – 19
87	2 Corinthians 13: 5	122	Mark 12: 29 – 31
88	Psalm 33: 1	123	Matthew 7: 21
89	Psalm 16: 7	124	Matthew 7: 21
90	Psalm 8: 2	125	Acts 1: 4 -5, 8
91	Luke 17: 20 – 21	126	Genesis 3: 1 – 6
92	Romans 8: 35 – 39	127	Nehemiah 9: 5
93	Psalm 63: 1 – 4, 8	128	Ecclesiastes 3: 1 – 8
94	Revelation 2: 1	129	Ecclesiastes 3: 11a
95	2 Corinthians 5: 20a	130	Jeremiah 29: 11
96	John 10: 27	131	Numbers 24: 10
97	1 Corinthians 14: 2	132	Numbers 25: 1 – 3 & 6
98	Proverbs 11: 21	133	Psalm 34: 7
99	Psalm 37: 25	134	Matthew 6: 19 – 21
100	Galatians 6: 9 – 10	135	John 10: 27 – 28
101	Isaiah 40: 28 - 31	136	Galatians 6: 28
102	Matthew 5: 6	137	Galatians 5: 7
103	Proverbs 3: 5 – 8	138	Galatians 5: 8 – 9
104	Numbers 23: 19	139	1 Corinthians 5: 7
105	Luke 9: 62	140	Romans 12: 2
106	Isaiah 40: 29 – 31	141	Proverbs 4: 18
107	See Ephesians 3: 20	142	Luke 5: 36 – 38

www.ingramcontent.com/pod-product-compliance
Lightning Source LLC
Chambersburg PA
CBHW030441010526
44118CB00011B/746